THE HEART OF
MYSTICISM

Writings by Joel S. Goldsmith

All titles listed above can be found at www.AcropolisBooks.com.

THE HEART OF MYSTICISM

VOLUME IV
THE 1957 INFINITE WAY LETTERS

Joel S. Goldsmith

Acropolis Books, Publisher
Longboat Key, Florida

THE HEART OF MYSTICISM:
VOLUME IV – THE 1957 INFINITE WAY LETTERS

© 2018 by Acropolis Books

Previously published as part of a compilation of years of
Infinite Way Letters from 1955 to 1959.

For information contact:
Acropolis Books, Inc.
Longboat Key, Florida
http://www.acropolisbooks.com

Book design by Palomar Print Design

Library of Congress Cataloging-in-Publication Data

Goldsmith, Joel S., 1892-1964.
The heart of mysticism: volume iv–the 1957 infinite way letters / Joel S.
Goldsmith.
      p. cm.
  ISBN 978-1-939542-75-5
  1. Spiritual Life. 2. New Thought. I. Title.

BP610.G64G651565 2007
299'.93—dc22   2007030700 CIP

Except the Lord build the house,
they labour in vain that build it.

Psalm 127

"Illumination dissolves all material ties and binds
men together with the golden chains of spiritual
understanding; it acknowledges only the leadership
of the Christ; it has no ritual or rule but the divine,
impersonal universal Love; no other worship than
the inner Flame that is ever lit at the shrine of Spirit.
This union is the free state of spiritual brotherhood.
The only restraint is the discipline of Soul; therefore,
we know liberty without license; we are a united
universe without physical limits; a divine service to
God without ceremony or creed. The illumined walk
without fear — by Grace."

From *The Infinite Way* by Joel S. Goldsmith

PREFACE

A mystic is an individual who has attained some measure of conscious awareness of God, one who lives a greater and greater portion of his or her experience in the presence and oneness of this Spirit and is prepared to be an instrument of expression and fulfillment of God's purpose.

Joel Goldsmith is considered by many to be one of the great Western mystics of the twentieth century. He felt strongly that those who were inwardly directed to discover this conscious awareness of the Presence of God could accelerate their progress through the active study and practice of specific spiritual principles. When this was coupled with the practice of meditation, he had the conviction this would inevitably lead to the mystical experience.

Beginning in 1954, Joel wrote a monthly *Letter* as a specific teaching tool for his students and felt this was his way of remaining in touch with those who sought his guidance in all parts of the world. He could not emphasize the importance of these *Letters* enough and stated in one of his final classes that:

> The books of the *Infinite Way Letters 1954*, '55, '56, '57, '58, '59 and then *Our Spiritual Resources* created from the *Letters* of 1960 and *The Contemplative Life* created from the *Letters* of 1961 are as important as any books we have, if not more so, because here you get in every chapter certain principles and their application so that you can always go to those books and find a working tool.

Although all of Joel's monthly *Letters* after 1959 were eventually published as individual books with specific titles, those considered among the most valuable—the 1954 through 1959 *Letters*—were not. Acropolis Books is pleased to present a six-volume collection of these invaluable *Letters* entitled *The Heart of Mysticism*. This reintroduction of these seventy-two monthly *Letters* is a part of our continuing commitment to ensure that all of Joel Goldsmith's writings remain available and accessible to interested readers now and in the future.

Acropolis Books, 2018

TABLE OF CONTENTS

THE INFINITE WAY LETTERS 1957

The Heart of Mysticism

VOLUME IV
The 1957 Infinite Way Letters

❖ 1 ❖

JANUARY

OUT OF DARKNESS—LIGHT[1]

> And the earth was without form, and void; and darkness was upon the face of the deep. And the Spirit of God moved upon the face of the waters. And God said, Let there be light: and there was light.
>
> Genesis 1: 2

THE LIGHT OF GOD, the light of spiritual wisdom, enters consciousness only in the degree of our own receptivity and devotion to it. It cannot force itself upon us, nor can it come to us in any greater measure than we, ourselves, permit. God is the full and complete brightness thereof, but it is for us to determine the measure of the light we shall receive. It is not enough to say, "I would like the wholeness of God," when our actions disprove such a statement. If we really wanted God above all things, we would provide sufficient opportunity for It to fulfil Itself in us, so that we could receive the fullness of God's light.

To a great extent many of us are still living in spiritual darkness. Although we may all have experienced God's grace in some slight measure, even though it be in as slight a measure as is one grain of sand compared with all the sands in the universe, nevertheless, we do not yet know the real meaning of grace. Darkness is upon the face of the deep so far as spiritual health, spiritual harmony, spiritual supply, spiritual relationships, and spiritual peace are concerned. In acknowledging that spiritual darkness reigns, however, we have arrived at that place in consciousness where we are ready to open ourselves to the influx of spiritual light.

1

There is a moment in your life and in mine when darkness is upon us, and we are without form and void. If, in that emptiness, we can become very still, we shall feel the atmosphere of God envelop us, filling our whole being with light. Then comes the assurance: "*I*² will never leave you, nor forsake you. *I* was with you before Abraham was, and although you have not known Me, *I* have known you."

Yet, even with such comforting assurance, you will be tempted, as was the Master. These temptations may seem to come to you from outside, but that will only be the appearance: The temptation is always within you. In the wilderness, the Master was tempted by Satan; but when he turned on the devil, the only Satan the Master found was the sense of a personal selfhood or personal ego. That was and is the only devil. It tried to tempt the Master to turn stones into bread, to seek a reputation in the world, to do something which would enable him to say, "How great a man am I," or "What great understanding I have"; but he recognized these three suggestions as temptations and resisted them: "Get thee behind me, Satan."

So it is that you may be faced with the temptation of poverty, disease, or sin; or you may be faced with the temptation to believe that someone is hating you as an individual or that someone is persecuting your nation, race, or religion. You may think that such temptations are coming to you from some devil out in the world, but that is not true. All temptation is within your own self; it is the personal self, tempting you to believe that there is a selfhood other than God's own Being, or that there is an activity or condition separate and apart from God.

In these periods of temptation, which are like unto the darkness or void upon the face of the earth, wait for God, Himself, to say, "Let there be light." In the silence, in stillness and quietness, let this light envelop you. Let it enfold you, illumining your life. Let its inner radiance, shining without, light not only your way, but the way of all who touch your consciousness.

When this light shines in your consciousness, all who are a part of your spiritual household partake of the spiritual light that comes through you. No spiritual teacher or seer has ever been the sole beneficiary of the light which he has received; he has been thrust out into the world that others might share in the benefits of his illumination.

> Ye are the light of the world. A city that is set on a hill cannot be hid.
>
> Neither do men light a candle, and put it under a bushel, but on a candlestick; and it giveth light unto all that are in the house.
>
> Let your light so shine before men, that they may see your good works, and glorify your Father which is in heaven.[3]

No one can keep the light of God bottled up within himself. This spiritual light makes us the light of the world, even if that world is limited to our own household.

The noise and confusion of the world obscure the light of God, but when we approach God in quietness and in confidence, peace steals into our souls; and then, in that moment of peace, the light of God, the light of spiritual wisdom and of healing, pours through and functions consciously within us. It may be revealed to us through a teacher, although it need not come through that channel; it can come directly from God into our consciousness. Eventually it must be so. A teacher can carry us only so far; from then on, through the spiritual light we have received from within, we must walk on the waters with no outside aid.

The whole message of The Infinite Way is for the purpose of showing the people of the earth how to make the transition from being a human being to being that man who has his being in Christ. It is a transition from a faith in the external to a complete faith in the Infinite Invisible. Too long have the people of the earth put their faith in princes; in armaments, the navies and air-fleets of the world; in money, gold taken from the earth, and then buried again in the earth. Too long have they depended upon *forms* of good.

The Ephemeral Nature of Form

All forms are temporal and eventually are outmoded. Everything has form. All substance must have form, although not always a form visible to the human senses. Even thought has form. The higher we rise in spiritual unfoldment, the more aware are we of spiritual form or spiritual reality. For example, we become less conscious of men and women as so many faces and figures, so many hats, dresses, suits, eyeglasses; and we are increasingly aware of the outer symbols that are the expression of the inner being—the look in the eyes or the smile on the lips. Then, there comes a stage in our realization of the spiritual nature of individual being when we rise above even that. New forms, new instruments, take the place of the old; yes, even old forms of body give way to the new. The body we had as an infant or at six years of age or at twenty is gone; and five years from now, we shall look in a mirror and see a different form from that which we see now.

New forms of treatment take the place of the old forms. You will note that every book and every manuscript in The Infinite Way writings have chapters on treatment and meditation. A hasty reading of these chapters may lead you to think that there are too many different forms of treatment for any one person to grasp. Some of them may even appear to be contradictory; but, as you study further, you will discover methods of treatment in The Infinite Way writings that are perfectly suited to where you are in consciousness at this particular moment, while other forms of treatment may seem completely foreign to your thought or ability. Remember, however, that these treatments are for each one of us at the particular level of consciousness in which they may find us. That does not mean that next week or next year you may not discard the treatment that seems so important to you now and see the wisdom of another kind of treatment illustrated in some other section of the Writings. You grow gradually from one form of treatment to another, one form of meditation to another; and in time you come to the place where only rarely is it necessary to remember some truth. Usually, truth is imparting itself to you continuously from the infinity of your being. Yes, every form—body, home, treatment, activity, relationships—is replaced by a new form; but throughout all the changing forms, God is continuously revealing Itself to us in new forms of life, higher forms, and higher and better ways of living.

There is nothing formed which God did not form. We sometimes fear that which has form because we forget that there is no power in the form itself: All power is in That which gave it form. Never fear a person; never fear a condition; never fear a circumstance: All power is in God, the Infinite Invisible. No weapon that is formed against us shall ever touch us, whether that weapon be in the form of a person, or bullets, or hatred, animosity, jealousy, or germs. Nothing that is formed shall have power, jurisdiction, or dominion over us if we stand firm in our faith in the Infinite Invisible.

We do not need anything or anybody that exists in the world of creation. Our entire need is for an inner contact with the Source of all that exists in this universe. When we have the Source, we have Its form. The Source will appear to us as the form of whatever is necessary in our experience—employment, inventions, home, family, or supply. These forms will come out of the void, out of the darkness; the Spirit of God will move on that darkness and void; and the light will come, revealing earth, water, sky, sun, moon, stars, fish, beasts, and birds—every moving thing that is upon the earth. We have no concern as the forms of creation come and as they go in our experience because we have the creative Principle of all creation. We may be moved from one home to another, one kind of work to another, one city to another, or one country to another. Our concern is never with the outer form our experience may take because the creative Principle will create new forms for us wherever we may be.

The light shines. The light shines within you now; it moves in and out of your Soul, your consciousness, your mind, your Spirit, your being, and your body. There was a moment when there was only darkness, when you were a human being in spiritual darkness—a void, an emptiness, a barrenness, an incompleteness. Then, out of the nothingness of the Infinite Invisible, upon the face of that darkness, upon the face of that void, the Spirit moves. It penetrates the denseness of human consciousness and takes form: "Let there be light, and there was light." Let there be water, and there was water; let there be earth, and there was earth. Let there be harmony, and there is harmony; let there be supply, and there is supply; let there be an infinity of good, and there is an infinity of good; let the brotherhood of man be established upon the earth, and the brotherhood of man is established on earth.

Let us surrender ourselves to God—surrender every day afresh our possessions, our health, our understanding. Then, out of the darkness and void within us, the Spirit of God moves, and there is light.

Meditating to Achieve a Conscious Awareness of the Presence of God

Our lives tomorrow will be the same as they are today; and next year will be but a repetition of this year, unless there is a change of consciousness, and unless we, individually and specifically, do something to bring about this change in our consciousness. Reading books about truth or hearing lectures on truth will have only a minor effect upon our experience: It is the practice of these truths that brings about the desired change of consciousness. If you devote one hour a day to the reading or study of truth, you are increasing your consciousness of truth in some degree. If, however, you devote an hour twice a day, you may be assured that you are thereby increasing your consciousness of truth measurably and immeasurably. When the time comes, however, that you are devoting three or four hours a day to the study and meditation of truth, then you are really bounding into a new and higher state of consciousness. Eventually, the day comes when even that passes, and you no longer need to set aside a specific time for study and meditation, because you have reached the place in consciousness where you are praying without ceasing. You will recognize when this time has arrived by your response to the things of the world. Every time you hear a news broadcast or see a newspaper headline heralding some un-fortuitous circumstance, you automatically turn away from it in the recognition that this, which you are hearing or reading, can exist only as a picture in the human mind and not as any part of God's kingdom. *In God's kingdom harmony reigns.* In such instant recognition, when you have learned automatically to reinterpret the pictures of sense which touch your consciousness, you are praying without ceasing, and yet you are doing it without consciously declaring the truth.

This was the high state of consciousness of the Master. He was living in such an exalted state of spiritual consciousness that when a woman pressed through the throng, she was healed by touching the hem of Jesus' robe without his even knowing that she was there. Without any conscious thought on his part, in that exalted state, she was healed. Remember, however, that it was the days and nights which Jesus had spent in the wilderness, his years of training and self-discipline, that lifted him into this high consciousness in which he did not recognize any error to be denied or treated. So it will be with you. When you reach the point where you are never aware of any form of error to treat or to deny, your treatments and your prayers will be wordless, and yet you will be treating and praying all the time.

God's power flows through individual you and me in proportion to our creating a vacuum, a silence through which it can flow. Therefore, you can see the importance of arranging your life so that time is allowed for these periods of silence. Let your first period be when you wake up at the beginning of your day. Before you get out of bed in the morning, spend at least five minutes in reaching the center of your own being, in feeling at peace with your inner self. In this way, you begin the day by establishing yourself in the Spirit even before you leave the warmth of your bed in the morning. Wait there in quietness and peace for the Spirit of God as It moves upon the face of the waters. In the calm that envelops you, feel the Spirit of God as It enters, not only your Soul, but also your body. Feel it right down to your finger-tips; feel it in your toes; feel the Spirit moving in every part of your body.

Everyone gets out of bed at some time or other, some earlier and some later: The hour is of no importance. What is important is that there is a period at the beginning of the day for five or ten minutes of silence, and that there are additional periods during the day and night for the realization of the Presence. Give thirty or sixty seconds at intervals throughout the day to stopping the clamour of mind and body, pausing for another realization or inflow of the Spirit. Everyone has one minute, five minutes, or ten minutes in which he is alone. Using these periods for this purpose is a matter of training and is made possible by the intelligent ordering of one's life.

It is not enough to feel the presence of God only once in the course of the day: You must carry the consciousness of the Spirit with you *throughout* the day. If you stop at frequent intervals to bring God to your conscious remembrance, it becomes a continuing awareness. It is in the silence and in that inner peace that the Spirit of God moves. But this peace is not something that comes to you of its own accord; you bring it about by your moments of silence. One minute, even thirty seconds, is enough if you pause many times a day to remind yourself: "God's life is my life"; or "God's law is the law unto my being"; or "God's wisdom is infinite." Any one of these reminders will be sufficient to re-establish you in the Spirit.

If you should encounter a law of infection or contagion or meet with any suggestion of discord, stop, even in the midst of the turmoil, to realize: "No, God's law is infinite; God's power is infinite; God's understanding is infinite"; or

"God's presence is infinite and ever with me." Whatever the situation that presents itself to you may be, turn from it in the remembrance of God's presence and power. The assurance may come in a reminder of God's grace forever flowing freely to us:

Thy grace is sufficient for me. I have thought that I had to labor, to struggle, and to plan for my future; but now I need no longer worry, plan, or take anxious thought. There is a divine grace at hand that provides a sufficiency of all things. Thy grace is sufficient for me. God's wisdom is sufficient for me, and in that all-sufficiency, I can never lack wisdom and guidance. God's wisdom fills me; God's love fills me; God's presence is sufficient for me.

Through grace, my heavenly Father feeds me—feeds me spiritually, clothes me spiritually, maintains and sustains me spiritually. Forever more, this grace of God will interpret itself to me in the forms, and as the forms, necessary to maintain and sustain me in abundance, in joy, and in gladness. My expectancy is of God. Thy grace, Thy gifts, Thy good, Thy love, Thy mercy, and Thy justice are my sufficiency; and, therefore, I do not look to man for any good thing.

God's grace is filling this space; God's grace is filling these hands; God's grace is filling this body with health and joy and peace and power and dominion and all good. God's grace is filling every moment with the divine Presence, which is love and life eternal. Whatever demand is made upon me is fulfilled through the grace of God and not because of my physical strength, nor because of any storehouses or barns I may possess, nor even by virtue of my own wisdom or understanding. Through grace, I am given everything necessary to fulfil every demand made upon me.

Grace is a continual realization of God as the source of all good. It does not look to man for anything; it looks to God alone and then lovingly accepts the good as it comes through those individuals chosen for the purpose. You will find that as you continue in this meditation on God's grace for three months, four months, five months, or six months, meeting every appearance of discord with that remembrance of God's grace as your sufficiency, you begin to feel God's grace coming into expression in your experience : Good comes to you that you had not humanly expected; a sense of well-being fills you with a joy that you had not humanly expected; a sense of well-being fills you with a joy that no man can take from you; and then you know that God's grace is sufficient for you.

It is essential that you become established in the Spirit every day, before you undertake the work of that day, whether in your household or in the business world. It is only then that you are insulated from the world, only then that you have overcome the world and can move in and out of it, unaffected by its changes. Learn to wait every morning in the darkness of silent receptivity until you feel the Spirit within you, until you feel this calm descend upon you, this peace embracing you with an invisible Robe that hides you from the world—the fears, hates, and jealousies of the world. Then, in these moments of silent meditation, you discover that your light is come and "the glory of the Lord is risen upon thee."

THE FRIENDLY ROAD[4]

This issue of *The Seeker* is devoted to the message of The Infinite Way. In July, we had the very great joy of a visit from Mr. Joel Goldsmith, who is the author of The Infinite Way teaching. Mr. Goldsmith was with us for three days and nights and he addressed nine separate meetings. ... It was a very wonderful experience for us all, bringing to us complete confirmation of the work of our fellowship for the past twenty-six years.

I had read the book, *The Infinite Way*, and some of the monthly *Letters* which are sent to Infinite Way students, but apart from this knew very little about the author or his message. Upon his arrival, I discovered that he had flown the four or five thousand miles from Sydney to Perth and back to keep his promised word. When he had promised to visit Perth, he thought it was sure to be somewhere near Sydney. When one reads a man's writings, it may be foolish, but it is very human to make a mental picture of him, and this I had done, only to find that I was completely wrong. He told us something of his own background and the absence of any racial or religious prejudice in it, a little of the spiritual awakening which came to him twenty-seven years ago, and of how it had changed the whole focus of his mind and life; for Paul's transformation from Saul to Paul was no more real than was his. His experience as a practising metaphysician for fifteen years, and the establishing of his own intuitive link with the Divine as the rock is a most fascinating story, which has resulted in a tremendously vital man who has, beyond doubt, grown in that consciousness until he is expressing in simple, clear terms what will be the message of the Kingdom and the Master for this age.

In introducing the message of The Infinite Way, I will not attempt to interpret it, but let the author and his books and the tapes explain it. I can, however, show how perfectly this message merges into the work of the Center and will try to do that. Twenty-six years ago, we took the New Testament Scriptures as the basis of our work, claiming the right to use our own awakened intuitive faculty as the interpreter, and we have been led progressively to understand the mission and message of the Master, and led to place the emphasis, firstly, upon the individual's need for faith in the infinite wisdom and love of God, secondly, upon freedom and responsibility for each one, and thirdly, upon the need for spiritual fellowship. The kingdom of God is within you, and the inwardness of Truth has always been the basis of our understanding, with the supreme test of love towards God and man as the measure of our growth.

We have always explained faith as the use of man's intuitive faculty, the innate capacity to know the truth which Peter used when he declared, "Thou art the Christ, the Son of the living God." That is the rock upon which Christ founded his group; flesh and blood could not know it, and it is upon this inner capacity which we have built, and are still building our work.

This awakening is worth waiting for, in fact, it is foolish not to wait until this inner link of knowingness is awakened; man can know beyond the level of his instincts or his intellect, when his intuition is quickened. Imagine then, if you can, the joy of our group when we heard this truth and concept made to live by Mr. Goldsmith. It is no wonder that our hearts burned within us as he revealed the rock upon which The Infinite Way was established, for it is the basis of our work, and we know it works that way.

Always we have been impressed to keep the doors of our hearts, and the Center open, and to resist any attempt to enclose us or to condition our minds. Often we have been tempted to become a little dogmatic, exclusive and smug, but we knew how contrary to the Spirit of Christ that would be. Imagine how we rejoiced when we heard Mr. Goldsmith inviting us to realize our freedom, by declaring, after locating the Presence within us, "Where the Spirit of the Lord is, there is liberty," meaning of course, freedom from every form of exclusiveness and human limitations and lack.

Humanity has surely been conditioned by the group or racial mind which automatically reflects the group concepts; so all true healing is to release man from the fixations of his flesh, and to teach him what he is, the Son of God. We have never felt led to become affiliated with any of the many groups in the metaphysical world, but we do accept and rejoice in being associated with The Infinite Way teaching, for it does indicate and teach the way in which man can be freed from all his fears, doubts, pride, hates, greeds, and inharmonies.

It is not easy to build up a group of individualists and maintain the spirit of true fellowship and the bond of peace, but that has been our ideal and aim, and the many thousands of our co-workers bear witness to the joy and power of fellowship in truth. I am not clear just where we are linked to the work of The Infinite Way in this concept of mental and spiritual agreement and harmony, but I do know that my own understanding and progress have been largely conditioned by my willingness and ability to keep flowing this spirit of fellowship and unity; and I do know that I was not in the presence of Mr. Goldsmith for many minutes before I experienced this wonderful sense of the fellowship of Spirit. The questions in my mind melted away, and I was content to relax and enjoy comradeship of soul with one who had become so identified with his message, that he was a living witness to its reality and truth.

Our interest in healing work is based upon the Gospels. We have accepted the Master's methods, and wherever there has been response and receptivity, there have been results; but this message of healing by teaching The Infinite Way, rather than the old one of teaching folk by healing them, is also in the Gospels, and it is only such healing that endures.

We have declared that we are Seekers, and find even after we have recognized the truth of God's presence within, we are still seeking to realize its fullness and power. The Master's statements, "Blessed are they who hunger and thirst after righteousness for they shall be filled ... Seek ye first the kingdom of God and His righteousness, and all these things shall be added unto you," to us, mean really that we are still seeking to put the Kingdom and its interests first. Often it happens we can know a truth or accept a statement as truth with our minds, but fail to apply it to our inner lives, and as long as that happens, we are seekers for the technique of application and realization.

We have sent to England for a number of Infinite Way books and they will be available in our library. Mr. Goldsmith is writing the leading article for this month's magazine, and all those who are interested, and that means all of us who are regular attendants at our Center will be given an opportunity to hear the tape recordings as they come to hand. We recognize that The Infinite Way message is worldwide in its application and appeal; we know that same law that applies to the individual consciousness applies to the whole world. We have been a rather isolated group, and it is good for us to get this larger, broader look at the world; it will surely make us wider between the eyes and deeper in our sympathies and loves.

To conclude, I can only say I have never before met anyone who was so absolutely sure of his link with God and good, or anyone who is so completely obedient to its direction, and it is that certainty and conviction which was such a real inspiration to all who heard his witness in Perth. I find that the Bible Society in Perth has sold out its New Testaments with the Master's words recorded in red ink, which Mr. Goldsmith suggested his hearers should use and read to become familiar with Christ's own words.

"Beloved, now are we the sons of God"—we have always been just that, but have failed to realize its full significance and implications. Recognizing the presence of God within, let us all now seek the full realization of its power, wonder, and freedom, and so extend our fellowship to all. We are each a unit of awareness and in that awareness is God. I am sure that I am speaking for all of the group in Perth when I say that the result of Mr. Goldsmith's visit has been to stimulate our will to know and understand; to increase our understanding of the indwelling reality of Christ; and to cause us to rejoice in the knowledge that the truth we have loved and been practicing in our own Center is being taken to the world through the activity of The Infinite Way and give thanks.

TRAVELOGUE

This message comes to you in January when the world looks hopefully forward to the New Year. The world has been doing this "hopefully looking forward" for countless thousands of years, and it has only attained bigger and better "morning after" headaches to show for these New Year's hopes. Why has the forward, hopeful look proved so frustrating? You already know the answer, but for "their sakes" I repeat: The world has sought peace, safety, security, prosperity, and health. It cannot find them. Many of us who embark on the spiritual path also seek healing and companionship and supply. And we cannot find them.

Let us seek and attain such a moment as was experienced by Saul of Tarsus on the road to Damascus, and we shall be transformed into a Paul, an apostle and a witness of Truth.

Believe me, when I tell you that I have walked the streets of Damascus, "the street which is called Straight,"[5] and have felt the illumination Paul carried with him into the city.

Seek the Spirit of the Lord, for where It is, there and there only, is peace on earth, plenty, and liberty. Seek the grace of God and prove for yourself that His grace is a sufficiency of *all* things needful in daily experience. When patients seek healing of a practitioner or spiritual healer, they seek that which they cannot receive. When they seek, through the illumined one, the realization of His presence, then health and supply are added unto them.

To be grateful for a healing is an error: Be grateful that the Spirit of God has been realized. To be grateful for a demonstration of supply or employment or home is more error: Be grateful that God's Spirit has been brought to your conscious awareness. Do not be grateful for the loaves and fishes you receive, but for the miracle of the principle that has been given you. The gift of God is Himself, and that Gift appears in as many forms of good as are necessary to our experience.

Be not hopeful of good for the New Year, but *assure* yourself of good by daily beginning your activities with a silent, inner realization of His presence, His grace.

There is nothing deeper in the spiritual literature of the world than the two words, *I AM*. As a matter of fact, when you are in the depths of despair, those are the only two words that can come to your rescue—not what I would *like* to be, not what I *hope* to be, not what I am *trying* to be through the use of all these words. In the end, you will realize this: Whatever it is I am seeking, I already am. You will then give up all this physical effort and mental effort. You will give up all the struggling. Why struggle for that which I already am?

Do not try to be more spiritual; do not try to be more moral; do not try to be more good; do not try to be more anything. Give up the struggle; stop trying to be one thing other than that which you now are; settle back and realize: That which I am, *I am. All that God is, I am. That which I am seeking, I am.*

If only you could stop living a minute from now, you would find yourself resting, content in this *nowness*. This is the only minute you will ever know. There will never be another minute beyond this minute. It is always this minute, and in this minute, I already *am*. In this minute, all that God is, I am. In this minute, all that the Father hath is mine. "For he that hath, to him shall be given: and he that hath not, from him shall be taken even that which he hath."[6] Therefore, any attempt to get more than you now have is going to fail, because all that God is, I am; and all that the Father hath is mine.

Acknowledging a lack is going to demonstrate a lack. Do you not see that anything you acknowledge is that which you must demonstrate? You can only demonstrate what you acknowledge: "I have a lack"; then, that is my demonstration. Do you see that? "I haven't enough"; again, that is my demonstration. Whatever I acknowledge as truth within me, that is what I must demonstrate.

If, on the other hand, I acknowledge: "I and the Father are one, and all that the Father hath is mine. God is; therefore, I am. All that God is, I am;" then the fullness of the Godhead bodily fulfils Itself as my individual being. Now, this minute, we are living in the fullness of time. Now, we are acknowledging the fullness of spiritual good. It is always now—this minute. Do you realize what a terrible tiling it would be to wake up to find that God could give you something tomorrow? You would hate God. What is wrong with today? Why is God withholding anything from us today that He could give us tomorrow? Why? Is it a punishment? Is God holding out a reward? What is God? An overgrown man? No, there is no such God. You are told in The Infinite Way writings that if you knew the nature of God, you would need no other teaching. That is true. It is only in the degree that we are entertaining orthodox concepts of God that we are what we are.

To merge silently, freed, into the stream of infinitude, is the greatest good of life. The two aims of the world's mysticism are here set forth: first, to find the eternal in given life, to feel the emanation of Spirit in every manifested thing; second, to take on the sense of the flow of Spirit, to bathe in consciousness of the stream of divinity, in union with the Soul and all souls.[7]

"Without me ye can do nothing." Listen, heed, watch—let Me through. Stillness, quietness, peace. I live over your shoulder— seeing, acting, doing, being. It is well. It is established. It is done.

❖ 2 ❖

MAJOR PRINCIPLES
OF THE INFINITE WAY[1]

IN JUNE OF 1947, *The Infinite Way* was released in book form in the United States. In the nine years that have passed since then, the message of The Infinite Way has found expression in more than twenty books which have been published in the United States in American editions; in England in British editions; in Holland in a Dutch edition; and in Switzerland in a German edition; besides which, many of the smaller pamphlets have been translated into Swedish and Danish, and are being translated into other languages.

We have watched the spread of this message into many countries around the globe. In the past two and a half years, it has been necessary for me to make four European trips, in addition, of course, to those to the American Continent and three trips around the world. I know that you will realize what takes place in our consciousness, as we behold this unfolding message finding its way into human consciousness in all parts of the globe without the benefit of organization, promotion, advertising, or memberships.

This message is placed before the world, and you, as an individual, have an opportunity, in one way or another, of reading or hearing it and finding whether or not this message brings a response from within your own being. If it does find a response within you, then this message is for you; and if

21

there is no inner response, it is not for you. Your function is to keep on searching and searching and searching for God, until the teaching or the teacher that awakens you to the realization of your true identity touches you.

Before I left my home in Hawaii for my latest globe encircling trip, I received an invitation to go to Sydney and Melbourne in Australia, and lo, and behold, by the time I had reached London, I had received more invitations from Adelaide and from Perth, and these I was more than happy to accept. It was in this way that I found myself one bright sunny morning in Perth, meeting Mr. Webb and finding a spiritual bond existing between us, instantaneously recognized by both of us.

The privilege was extended to me to speak nine times in three days to the students at the Seekers' Center and to meet there many of Mr. Webb's students and friends.

In the course of my nine talks, I tried to sum up as briefly as possible the major principles of The Infinite Way so that students might understand why The Infinite Way came into existence and exactly what function it performs in the world. Surely, there is not a need for a new religion, nor is there a need for a new teaching. But if you will look around you in the world, read the newspapers, or listen to the radio for just a little while, I am sure you will agree that there is a need for understanding the great spiritual messages that have been given to us over a period of several thousand years by the greatest masters of all times. It is unfortunate that these teachings have become so over-organized that the message and the principles embodied in the message are lost. Therefore, every few centuries another teacher arises to sum them up, to rewrite them in the language of his day, and to call attention again to the fact that it is only in proportion as we know the truth that the truth can set us free. The Infinite Way restates the ancient wisdoms to this age in modern language and as a demonstrable principle.

Many wonder why, with all the truth messages that are in the world, there is still sin, disease, death, wars, lack and limitation on earth. The answer is very clear. We are told, "Ye shall know the truth, and the truth shall make you free." The question is: Do we know the truth? Do we know the *principles* of truth? Do we understand the *laws of God?* And over and above all, do we *know* God, whom to know aright is life eternal?

Right here you have one of the major principles of the message of The Infinite Way, so let us begin to see if, within the limits of this article, we cannot sum up for you these major principles, so that, as you read them, you will know whether or not they bring forth a response within you to encourage you to go further in your study of this particular teaching.

The Infinite Way reveals that the Christ-experience is a present possibility. This means, literally, that each one of us, in proportion to his devotion to the search, may achieve some measure of that mind which was also in Christ Jesus. What happens, when we attain a measure of spiritual consciousness, is this: The Christ takes over our experience and acts as a power, performing that which is our work, drawing to us the persons, things, supply, opportunities, activities, rewards, and recognition necessary to our daily life. You will remember that Paul said, 'I live, yet not I, Christ liveth my life," and in that quotation you will find the experience that actually happens when the Christ is realized in our consciousness. You will recall that in Scripture we are reminded that "he performeth the thing that is appointed for me." There again is the reminder that this Presence *once realized* does take over our experience—guides us, governs us, rules us, leads us, supplies us, maintains us, and sustains us throughout all our life. As a matter of fact, the realization of the Christ once achieved always goes before us to make the crooked places straight. It provides the manna for our daily needs. Always there is this It which is ever with us, which ever goes before us, which illumines us and keeps us on the spiritual path of harmony, wholeness, completeness, and perfection.

The Nature of God

Probably the very deepest teaching in the message of The Infinite Way is on the subject of the nature of God. Perhaps you think that you know God. Perhaps you believe that the synonyms for God which you have studied really constitute an understanding of God, but this is not so. If once we attain a knowledge of the nature of God, we shall at the same time understand that man is the Son of God, and we shall understand the nature of prayer which unites us with all the presence and all the power of God.

Do not be surprised when I say to you that once you realize the nature of God, you will never again pray to God in the way that men ordinarily do pray.

Since God is not a giving God or a withholding God, it is never necessary to ask God for anything. More especially, since God is Spirit, it would indeed be a waste of time to ask God for something of a material nature. The Master, Christ Jesus, revealed that, when he said, "Take no thought for your life, what ye shall eat, or what ye shall drink; nor yet for your body what ye shall put on."[2] He told us something of the nature of God when he said, in effect, that God is divine intelligence, "Your Father knoweth that you have need of these things"; and then he told us more of the nature of God when he implied that God is divine love by adding, "for it is your Father's good pleasure to give you the kingdom."³

Here you see two aspects of the nature of God. One is that God is divine intelligence and, therefore, there is never any need for you to tell God what things you have need of, nor to attempt to influence God to give you these things since God is not withholding them, for it is His good pleasure to give you the kingdom. Once you recognize God as infinite Intelligence and divine Love, the whole nature of your prayer will change. This, you, yourself, will realize as you learn to approach God, not in the nature of a power that you would beseech for favors or ask for gifts, but rather in the knowledge that you can rest in that same realization in which David rested when he was enabled to say, "The Lord is my shepherd, I shall not want."⁴ Do you not see that calm and certain assurance: "The Lord *is* my shepherd, I shall not want"? No need there to beseech God, to ask or to beg of God, but rather to abide in the awareness that *He leadeth* me beside the still waters, *He maketh* me to lie down in green pastures.

The Master further revealed the nature of God, when, to John's question, "Art thou he that should come?" he answered: "Go and shew John again those things which ye do hear and see: The blind receive their sight, and the lame walk, the lepers are cleansed, and the deaf hear, the dead are raised up, and the poor have the gospel preached to them."⁵ This, then, is the nature of God, that man should be alive, eternally so, immortally so, and never know death, since the Master in raising the dead proved that death is never the will of God for man. Therefore, man could rise above the need for death. And, of course, it was God's will that man be eternally well, since Christ Jesus said that he came to do the will of the Father, and the will of the Father was that the sick be healed. So you see that God's will is that we be well, and therefore, the nature of the Christ is to restore us to our God-given heritage of health, abundance, and life eternal.

You will always know a Christly man or woman because those who touch them on life's highway find life eternal, health, and wholeness, and receive spiritual blessings through their contact with these men and women.

The Nature of Prayer

To understand the nature of God in this way and to understand the Christ-mission must, of course, reveal to you the nature of prayer. Now, you can no longer pray for anything, but must confine your prayers to asking, seeking, and knocking for spiritual wisdom, spiritual guidance, spiritual bread, wine, and water. When you learn to turn to the Father for the revelation of God in your experience—for the actual demonstration of God in your experience—then, and only then, are you beginning to understand the nature of prayer.

It is important while studying the nature of prayer to read the New Testament very carefully and to note that the Master makes it more important that we pray for our enemies than that we pray for our friends. There is a reason for this. You see, understanding and forgiveness are two of the major qualities of Christ-consciousness. For this reason, the Master taught that we are to forgive seventy times seven and that we must forgive our enemies, those who oppress us and those who hate us and despitefully use us. And so until we learn to pray for our enemies and to forgive them, we are really not praying in the sense of prayer as revealed by the great Master.

As you read what I am saying to you about the nature of God, the nature of the Christ-mission, and the nature of prayer; it is almost certain that you are pausing at the end of every paragraph to read over again what is written and probably to weigh the meaning of what you have read. If so, you are beginning to meditate, to ponder, and to dwell on truth and in truth; you are obeying the Ninety-first Psalm: "He that dwelleth in the secret place of the most High," and to him, of course, come none of earth's tragedies. While you are thus pondering within yourself the nature of God, the nature of Christ, and the nature of prayer, you are dwelling in God. In the same way, in the fifteenth chapter of John— and I hope that you will read that entire chapter—you will notice that it says that if you abide in Me and if you let this Word abide in you, then you are one with the vine, and the vine is one with the Godhead, and so all good is flowing to you, and you will bear fruit richly. Now, as you are pondering these truths, you are abiding in the word of God; you are letting the word of God abide in you and, of course, you may be assured of this: It will not be long before you, too, will be bearing fruit richly.

You see, now, that the next form of prayer is pondering the word of God or meditating upon the word of God, which really means abiding in the Word and letting the Word abide in you and dwelling in the secret place of the most High.

Continuing to dwell on the subject of God, the nature of God, you come to a really remarkable place in your experience. One day it will dawn upon you: God *is*! It will dawn on you with such certainty and with such clarity that almost instantly all fear of man whose breath is in his nostrils, and all fear of human conditions and circumstances will drop away from you. Perhaps you have not realized that up to this time, you have not been quite certain that God *is*. No one, no one at all, can *ever* entertain a fear or a doubt once the certainty is realized that *God is*.

This type of prayer and meditation leads to an actual conviction that *God is*. Here you have all that is necessary for the re-establishment of divine harmony in your experience. All discord comes from the belief that God is not, or that God is not functioning in our particular experience, or that for some reason we have become separated from God. Once you realize that *God is*, all anxiety and concern drop away from you, because the very nature of God makes it an impossibility for you to be in any place where God is not. Now, you begin to understand the meaning of such passages as: "The place whereon thou standest is holy ground,"[6] or "If I make my bed in hell, behold thou art there,"[7] or "Yea, though I walk through the valley of the shadow of death, I will fear no evil: for thou art with me."[8] So you are led to see, not only that God is, but that *God is omnipresence* right where you are. *Right where you are*, "the place whereon thou standest is holy ground." Isn't that wonderful to know?

Again Scripture informs us: "Thou wilt keep him in perfect peace, whose mind is stayed on thee[9] ... My presence shall go with thee, and I will give thee rest."[10] Are you beginning to suspect now that this is just what we have been doing almost from the first paragraph of this article?

We have been keeping our mind stayed on *God* and on His Son, the Christ, the Spirit of God in man. We have been acknowledging *God* as the only presence, the only power, as omnipresence and omnipotence, *right where I am*.

Is it not clear to you, now, as you sit here reading and pondering these passages of Scripture and dwelling in thought on the nature of God, of the Christ, and of prayer, that you are actually praying, meditating, acknowledging Him in all your ways, keeping your mind stayed on God, staying in the Word and letting the Word abide in you, and that you are really fulfilling Scripture at this very moment? This is what the metaphysical world would call giving yourself a treatment. Actually, it is much more than that. It is *abiding in God*. It is living and moving and having your being in this very truth of God, and it is fulfilling that great passage: "Ye shall *know* the truth, and the truth shall make you free."[11] You are knowing the truth about God, knowing the truth about the Christ, knowing the truth about the activity of God in your individual experience, knowing the truth about your relationship to God.

Our Relationship to God

Just see what an important message now opens up to us as we begin to ponder our relationship to God, and as we do that, let us keep in thought, of course, that our authority at the moment is Christ Jesus and the New Testament. And what does that authority teach us? We are children of God and as children, heirs, and as heirs, joint-heirs. Isn't this something really important to know about our relationship to God—that we *are* sons, that we *are* heirs, and, therefore, we can say as it says in Scripture, "Son, thou art ever with me, and all that I have is thine."[12] Do you not feel the release from worldly cares which that passage gives? Do you not feel an assurance in that stated relationship that exists between us and our Father? The Master not only spoke of his Father within him, but he said *your* Father and *my* Father. And he also said that you are to call no man on earth your father, but that *one* is your Father, the Father in heaven. There again you have this relationship of Father and son, heir, joint-heir.

The message of The Infinite Way from beginning to end is a constant dwelling on the nature of God; the nature of individual being, your being and mine; the nature of the Christ-mission, which is, of course, the mediator between God and our individual experience; the nature of prayer, meditation, and communion that binds us all together in the divine relationship of oneness.

Remember the significance of the message: "I and my Father are *one*."[13] It is in this relationship that we find our good revealed in the message of The Infinite Way. Because of our oneness with God, all that the Father hath is ours, and therefore, we can truthfully say that infinity, eternality, immortality, wholeness, completeness, and perfection are *mine now*, not by virtue of myself, but by virtue of my *oneness* with God. Whether or not at the moment our good is evident, that is, evident through the five physical senses, we can, through spiritual discernment, declare that in our oneness with God, our eternal and immortal harmony is forever established.

Cast Your Bread

Now you can understand why we are told to cast our bread upon the waters. You can also understand why the Hebrew master asked the widow what she had in the house, and you know of her good fortune because she answered, "a few drops of oil." Because of her answer, he could tell her to begin to pour, and as she began to pour, the cruse of oil never ran dry. So with us, as we learn to cast our bread upon the waters, beginning, if necessary, with just the few drops of oil that we have or the few loaves and fishes, we soon learn that all of this multiplies itself. "For he that hath to him shall be given: and he that hath not, from him shall be taken even that which he hath."[14]

So we learn from that the lesson of supply. The very moment that we declare, "I have not," or "I have an insufficiency," that is what we begin to demonstrate. But in the moment that this is reversed, and we understand, "Son, thou are ever with me, and all that I have is thine," we begin to cast our bread upon the waters, to pour those few drops of oil, to break those few loaves and fishes, to let loose of that which we know we possess, and watch the law of multiplication come into operation. This was the vision of the great mystical poet, Browning, when he said, "Truth is within ourselves and we must open out a way for the imprisoned splendour to escape." If truth is within ourselves, so is the bread, the wine, the meat, and the water within us. Do you not see, then, that instead of asking God for these things, it is only necessary that we open out a way to use the amount that we already have within us and watch as it multiplies itself in going out.

You will find that, in the message of The Infinite Way, the subject of supply is a most interesting one because you will learn that you cannot demonstrate supply. You must realize that supply already abides in its fullness within you, and the only way that you can enjoy abundant supply is by beginning to cast your bread upon the waters, pouring the few drops of oil that you have, beginning to break the few loaves and fishes; and, then, watch this truth multiply them.

Prayer and meditation begin with pondering, declaring, reading, and remembering the word of God, and these activities lead to a much higher unfoldment on the subject of prayer. Through the development of your consciousness, you ultimately come to a place where you recognize that the word of God is the real and the highest form of prayer, and that this form of prayer is something that you do not utter, but something to which you become receptive. Then you find yourself living constantly in a state of receptivity to what is called "the still small voice" that is within you and which is *always* ready to declare itself to you, in proportion as you learn to be still and hear the voice within.

Truth is first of all consciously known, consciously read, and consciously declared, until there comes a transition in your consciousness through receptivity, and then truth imparts itself to you from within you: Life imparts itself; love imparts itself; and supply imparts itself—*all from within you*—from your spiritual consciousness to your outer awareness.

It is in this way that you begin to perceive spiritually the nature of your own being and for the first time become aware of the fact that you are infinite. As you come to this place in consciousness, a whole new world opens to you, and forever after, you live without desiring anything, wanting anything, seeking anything, but always experiencing complete fulfillment every moment from within your own being.

The Healing Principle

The Infinite Way stresses the subject of spiritual healing. In that regard, we follow the Master in his statement that the Christ-mission is to heal the sick and raise the dead. We, too, believe that the understanding of God builds for us a healing consciousness through which we are able to bring health, harmony, wholeness, and completeness into the lives of those of our fellow-men and women who really seek a spiritual order of life. The mission of the Master shows how foolish it is to believe that we can live in the kingdom of God and yet experience all the trials and tribulations of the world. You will remember that he prayed that his disciples be in the world, but not of it.

Healing can be accomplished in proportion as we understand God to be one power, one presence, one law. In that understanding of oneness and, of course, the infinity of God being taken for granted, there cannot be two powers or two laws or two substances or two conditions. On every hand in the human picture, we are faced with the belief of material power, infection, contagion, heredity, and other suggestions of a power apart from God.

It is because we are faced every day with appearances of sin, sickness, death, lack, and limitation that such messages have come to earth as the Christ-message, truth-messages, The Infinite Way message. We are always dealing with appearances of evil in our experience. So it is that the healing consciousness restores harmony, not by appealing to God to remove anything or by using God as a weapon over negative conditions, nor by accepting the belief that there is a God that actually does overcome the earth's discords; but rather by coming into the understanding that God is the one and only power, and that this one Power makes all other claims of power null and void.

Coming into the awareness of the infinite nature of God as Love makes it virtually impossible for there to be a condition apart from God. Standing fast in this *oneness with God*, we find the negative appearances disappearing—not because God has healed or removed them, but because, through the realization of the presence of Truth, these negative appearances have been revealed as nothingness, as universal beliefs without substance, without cause, without law, and therefore, without effect.

Christ-Consciousness

Christ-consciousness is built entirely on the realization that Spirit *alone* is power, presence, and law. There is no such thing as a Christ-consciousness which embodies within it two powers or two laws or two conditions. Christ-consciousness is the consciousness of God as *one* and that one, omnipresent, good.

Spiritual consciousness, Christ-consciousness, the healing consciousness—such a consciousness is the realization of only *one* Power and enables you to say even to Pilate, "Thou couldest have no power at all against me, except it were given thee from above,"[15] or to say to a crippled man, "Rise, take up thy bed, and walk."[16] In other words, there is no power but God; therefore, stop fearing this negative sense. Stop hating this evil condition. Stop condemning this false appearance and begin to rejoice that your names are written in heaven and that, therefore, all these negative appearances are nothingness, without presence, without power, without law, without cause.

Do you not see now that as you continue to abide in this word of God, in this realization of God as one Power and one Presence, that you yourself are rising higher in consciousness to that place where the fears of this world, the sins of this world, and the evils of this world no longer come into your consciousness, and, therefore, no longer are reflected in your experience.

The Mystical Teaching of the Master

This brings us now to the great mystical teaching of The Infinite Way through which we demonstrate a state of consciousness which is a constant source of peace and joy to us. There is a peace that passeth understanding, and it is possible for us to attain this peace even in the world of discord that appears to be about us.

"My peace I give unto you: not as the world giveth,"[17] but rather *My* peace. This is a promise that within us there is this *My* peace which is the Christ-peace, given to us even before the world began. Our reliance now is not on some thing or some condition or upon some person in the outer world; but here and now, in this very instant, we transfer our faith and confidence from the outer world to a Withinness—that which within ourselves is *My* peace, a peace that is not the peace that the world can give us, but a peace that only the Christ can bestow. Through this, we begin to understand the meaning of the words of the Master: "I have meat to eat that ye know not of,[18] [and if you ask me, I] would have given thee living waters."[19] It is in this mystical revelation that we find that there is, within our own consciousness, a source of life which really is the source of our spiritual meat and bread and wine and water.

Through this understanding, we know what the Master meant when he said, "I will never leave thee, nor forsake thee[20] ... I am with you alway, even unto the end of the world."[21] Now we know that we have been given, within ourselves, the Christ-presence which is a "peace, be still" to all of earth's storms and, as we learn to listen for this inner voice, we hear it; and when we do, we remember, "he uttered his voice, the earth melted."[22] And so when we become conscious of that still, small voice within us, when we are consciously aware of the presence of that *I* within us which will never leave us nor forsake us and when we become consciously aware of *My* peace, the Christ-peace, within us, then do we know that He has uttered His voice within us, and the whole of earth's errors melt and disappear.

Only remember this: We must not permit ourselves to be brought back to the place where we believe in *two* powers, not even to where we believe that God is a power over evil, but rather we must know that because of God's all-power, evil is not a power.

Let me give you some passages from Scripture that should be memorized and should be remembered whenever we are faced with any appearance of a presence or power apart from God. In the realization of these truths and in the assurance which comes to us as we remember them, all negative forms disappear right before our eyes, and divine harmony is quickly realized:

> For I the Lord thy God will hold thy right hand, saying unto thee, Fear not; I will help thee.
>
> When the poor and needy seek water, and there is none, and their tongue faileth for thirst, I the Lord will hear them, I the God of Israel will not forsake them.
>
> I will open rivers in high places, and fountains in the midst of valleys: I will make the wilderness a pool of water, and the dry land springs of water.[23]

Remembering these inspired words will bring us back again to conscious union with God, because they will establish us as a branch connected with the vine, which in its turn is rooted and grounded in the Father—God, the husbandman.

Holding fast to these passages keeps us in the consciousness of God's presence, and, thereby, we learn and demonstrate that, "where the Spirit of the Lord is, there is liberty."[24]

TRAVELOGUE

This message will have to begin at the end and work backwards. And why not? It is easier for me to begin with today—right where I am—and go back in memory over the route from Texas to Oklahoma; New York; Vancouver and Victoria, Canada; Portland, Oregon; and then end in Seattle where we started the last half of our journey.

So today, as I am looking at the stacks of Christmas cards and New Year's greetings, piled high on my desk, I am wondering how I can say "Thank you" in some way that will really convey to each one of you the deep sense of gratitude I feel. It is December 20th, and already, actually more than 2,000 of you have written holiday greetings and sent letters and cards of appreciation for The Infinite Way and for the monthly *Letter*. Can you not easily believe that my heart and my Christmas stocking are very full? Please *feel* my thanks to you.

While I am on the subject of gratitude, may I tell you of my Christmas experience of 1956? It is my custom every year to meditate for several hours each day, culminating in an eight-hour meditation, beginning on Christmas Eve and extending into the morning. The purpose of this communion is to take our students into communion with God so that they may receive an impartation of a spiritual nature, especially befitting the need of the moment. The message to be given to all our students came early this week, and this is it:

At Christmas time, the world seeks to fulfil itself through the giving and receiving of material gifts. In like manner, spiritual students, forgetting that God is Spirit, go to God expecting some form of material or physical good, and thereby miss their demonstration. It will help you to pray aright if you will remember that the Master taught: "My kingdom is not of this world. ... I have overcome the world. ... My peace give I unto thee ... not as the world giveth, give I unto thee."

I know this will lift you as it has me.

Now back to our travelogue. Last month, I told you of the important teaching we received in Chicago and Seattle when the "still small voice" talked to me and through me while in the midst of class, giving us the secret of the cause and foundation of all error as revealed in Genesis in the explanation of the reason for the expulsion of Adam and Eve from the Garden of Eden: *They accepted the knowledge of good and evil.* To dispel all forms of error from our experience, it is necessary to withdraw all labels of good and evil. Call no man or thing good, for only God is good; call no man or thing evil, for God is infinite Spirit.

Then followed the secret of the Sermon on the Mount where we learn that although the *law* teaches "an eye for an eye"—the taking up of the sword, the indulging of human sense—*grace* is attained by refraining from the law and abiding in the spiritual Presence.

In Portland, Oregon, these subjects continued to develop, with students travelling along with us from many parts of the United States and Canada—students who were in Chicago and Seattle, and who again joined us in New York after the Victoria and Vancouver work with our students.

In Canada, we really received a surprise. It had been over two years since the last visit there, and this time we were greeted by several hundred students—a magnificent tribute from our cousins across the border. I cannot help but wish that all the world might look in on us as we sit with our groups of students in Canada, England, Holland, Sweden,

Germany, Africa, and Australia, and witness the joy and love that exist when we meet together in spiritual oneness.

After Canada, an unusual class came forth in New York, and while there, Harper and Brothers released my new book, *The Art of Meditation*. Three lectures and an autograph party sent the book winging on its way. I expect fine things of it because its companion book, *Practicing the Presence*, is having a runaway sale, and the comments are magnificent.

From New York I flew to Tulsa, Oklahoma, for a few days with good friends; then on to Brownwood and San Antonio, Texas, giving lectures for students from many surrounding cities. This was my first Infinite Way experience in Texas, and a most happy one.

Then, home to Hawaii and Christmas under palm trees and on sunny beaches—a strange Christmas for a New Yorker, but a delightful one.

The Easter of Our Lives is to be ready for distribution in the United States in February. For the benefit of those who do not know it, *The Easter of Our Lives* was an actual experience which took place Easter Week, several years ago in Seattle. While standing on the platform about to begin a lecture in the Seattle Truth Center, this vision appeared, and from my lips came the message of *The Easter of Our Lives*.

At present, there are no further plans for travel. I shall be at home until further notice but expect to make a short trip to Europe when George Allen & Unwin release the British edition of *The Art of Meditation*.

⁂ 3 ⁂

MARCH

UNDERSTANDING THE BODY

THE SECRET OF LIFE is right identification. Right identification changes your life the very moment that you have a conscious awareness of your true identity and begin to embody it, the very moment that you recognize and realize:

I am life eternal. I do not have to get knowledge of eternal life from a book: A book will not make my life eternal. I do not have to go to man whose breath is in his nostrils to learn something that will give me more life, youth, or vitality. No, all that any book or any man can do for me is to teach me that I already am that which I am seeking. That which I am seeking, I am; all that God is, I am because "I and my Father are one."[1]

The moment we realize: "I am life eternal; I am pure Spirit, pure consciousness," the question immediately arises, "But what about this body?" This is a mystery that has heretofore been unexplained. With the exception of the writings of The Infinite Way, there is no literature in the world which I have ever discovered that discusses this subject thoroughly. It is one of the deep mysteries of the philosophical and spiritual world. Attempting to arrive at a satisfactory understanding of this subject through the intellect is almost an impossibility, due to the fact that the subject of body deals with contradictions, not only the contradictions found in philosophical and spiritual literature, but contradictions in Scripture as well. Nobody who has tried to resolve these contradictions through the mind, that is, through the reasoning faculties or the intellect, has ever been able to come to any kind of a satisfactory conclusion. The explanation of this enigma came to light in my consciousness during a closed class, and it came flowing out by pure inspiration. I knew nothing about it until that minute when it poured out. I was not consciously aware even of having known all the passages of Scripture that came pouring out with it. It is this revelation that I would share with you in this *Letter*. If you can grasp it, this will be the most important lesson you will have learned in the message of The Infinite Way.

There are students of metaphysics who deny that they have a body; but if I am, then I must be *embodied*—I must have a body. I cannot exist as a cloud drifting about in the air, and even if I were a cloud floating in the air, that, too, would have form and body. But I do have a body. I am embodied, and my body is the temple of the living God. This is Scripture: "Know ye not that your body is the temple of the Holy Ghost. ..."[2]

Let us think for a moment about the conception of a child. As life, the child existed before conception. Where? How? That is not given us to know at this present moment, except through mystic perception; but we do know that somewhere, somehow, life existed, and, at a certain moment, it became visible to our awareness. As we look at that infant form, we can say, "Ah yes, that form is not your life because I can remember when that form was not there; so this is not *you.* This is your *form.* There is a "you" separate and apart from this form and there is a "you" that has form invisible to my sight." Such recognition is right identification. The infant is life; life constitutes the infant; and that life has form capable of propagating itself. We know now that that which we are seeing as body represents our view or our concept of that body. The mother's concept may be entirely different from our concept—mothers have been known to say that their newborn child was a beautiful baby; and yet, to most of us, newborn babies are not beautiful. The mother does not know that because she is looking at the child through different eyes; she is seeing *her concept* of her baby, and we are seeing the *universal concept* of baby.

We See Our Concept of Body

So it is with all of us. We look out upon each other and we see forms which we call bodies. A husband, looking at his wife, or a wife, looking at her husband, may see something entirely different from that which we see; a mother and father may see their son or daughter as something quite different from what the brother or sister may see as each other, or the way in which we may see one or the other of them as our friend. It is the same body, the same form. Is it? No, in each case, what we are seeing represents our concept of that which is there.

In accordance with universal belief, we replace one concept of body with another. As an infant, we had a body which we exchanged for the body of a child; when we outgrew that body, we exchanged it for the body of youth; still later, that body gave way to the body of the adult, which contained within itself a new function—the power to reproduce itself. That power was not in our infant body; it was not in our childhood body. But, as we advanced in years, we found that the power to become parents left us, because it was no longer a necessary function of our experience to be parents. Then we were ready to go on to different modes of life. So we look back and we see ourselves give up our dolls and toys; and, then, marbles, baseball, football, and school books; and, finally, we leave behind parenthood. Each time, as a function of our life drops away, we leave a part of our body behind and acquire a different concept of body and with it a different role in life.

You must come to the point where you understand your body and its function in your life; you must understand that *you* are not this *body*, and this *body* is not *you*: This body is an *instrument* through which you are functioning. You are the life of the body; you are the soul of the body; you are the intelligence of the body. You are that which uses the body as an instrument for your activities. You are that which walks or writes or paints or buys or sells, but the body is the instrument for the performance of that activity, and it is always obedient to you.

Rightful Place of Body

The body is the master of the person who lives in a material state of consciousness. Such a person seems to have no control over the body, but is controlled by it and by the bodily functions. The moment one rises to that point where he can perceive spiritual light, he begins, in some measure, to possess his body; he governs his body; he begins to use his body as he wishes to use it. The body, then, takes its rightful place as his servant instead of his master.

We do not love the body; we do not hate the body; we do not fear the body; we do not think of the body as ugly or beautiful; we do not think of the body as something to be put off. It is only the erroneous concept of the body which we entertain that is continuously giving us either pleasure or pain. It should not give us pleasure and it should not give us pain. Let us relegate the body to its proper place as an instrument for our activity. It is our vehicle for expression, just as an automobile is a vehicle for our transportation. We use our automobile, but we do not spend all our time admiring its bright color or polish and we are not too concerned if it gets a bit of mud on it. We keep it as clean as we can and see that it has proper lubrication. Just so should the body be used. Keep it clean, neat, and well-groomed; feed it wisely; respect it as the temple of the living God.

Remember, the body itself is as spiritual as we are. This form which we see is a mental concept of that body. It is merely a concept of that which is. If this which you see with your eyes *were* what it *is*, then it would always be what it is and would never change—never be young or old, sick or well. It is only because it is a concept of what it is that it changes. One day it seems healthy and one day sick, one day young and one day old, one day pretty and one day ugly, and all depending on what? On it? No, on what our view of it is. We are never seeing the body; we are seeing a human concept of body.

Flesh as Spiritual Identity

And without controversy great is the mystery of godliness: God was manifest in the flesh, justified in the Spirit, seen of angels, preached unto the Gentiles, believed on in the world, received up into glory.[3]

The mystery of godliness is what? God was manifest in the flesh:

I *appear as body; I function through body; I am seen in the world as body, but I am not seen. I am seen in the world as* body. I *am seen in the world as flesh.*

The Master's entire message and mission was to teach us that we are the children of God. "I and my Father are one[4] ...

he that seeth me seeth him that sent me."[5] He was careful
to include us in this relationship with God, because always
he said, "My Father and *your* Father." The Master knew
that his teaching was of no value if it set him apart from
the rest of the world. Of what value would his teaching and
example be if he were something that God sent to earth for
the purpose of teaching something that we were not able to
live up to? "I came forth from the Father, and am come into
the world. ..."[6] We are immaculately conceived; our birth, as
well as our mission, is that of the children of God. We are
not mortal flesh as we seem to be. The mystery of godliness
is God incarnate as your individual being and mine. God
manifest in the flesh means that God constitutes individual
selfhood, that God is the life, substance, and the very form
of our true being.

As you consciously live with the idea that God constitutes
individual being—your being—and that God is responsible
for your supply, your activity, and your success, you gradually
begin to lose the sense of personal selfhood. More and more
you realize that the responsibility rests upon God. Then it is
that you turn to the Source of all good, the creative Principle,
the Father within, that God may reveal Itself and Its plan.

Everything has its basis in the Invisible which appears
visibly and tangibly. As you begin to comprehend that fact,
you will see that creation is the act of an invisible Principle,
visibly manifest, God incarnating Itself as manifest form,
not the form you see with your eyes, but spiritual form. The
Master's words were: "And call no man your father upon the
earth: for one is your Father, which is in heaven."[7] God is the
creative principle of this universe appearing in infinite form
and variety, manifesting Itself visibly as individual being.
Therefore, the mystery of godliness lies in knowing that God
is our Selfhood: God is your Self; God is my Self.

The subject of flesh or body has always been a puzzle to the world, and great perplexity arises on this point: Where do flesh and body fit into the spiritual scheme? In Scripture, we find these words on the subject of flesh:

Flesh and blood cannot inherit the kingdom of God.[8]
There shall no flesh be justified in his sight.[9]
No flesh shall have peace.[10]
All flesh shall perish together ...[11]
Their flesh shall consume away while they stand upon their feet.[12]
For if ye live after the flesh ye shall die ...[13]
All flesh is grass, and all the goodliness thereof is as the flower of the field: The grass withereth, the flower fadeth: because the spirit of the Lord bloweth upon it ...[14]
The flesh profiteth nothing.[15]

In the same Scripture are such seemingly conflicting statements as:

Yet in my flesh shall I see God.[16]
I will pour out my Spirit upon all flesh ...[17]
And the glory of the Lord shall be revealed and all flesh shall see it together ...[18]
And all flesh shall see the salvation of God.[19]
Let all flesh bless his holy name forever and ever.[20]

And here is the greatest scriptural passage of all time on this subject:

And the Word was made flesh, and dwelt among us.[21]

In order to understand the subject of flesh and body, we must understand the meaning of these apparently contradictory passages, which are not contradictory at all when their true meaning is discerned. Spiritually, the word "flesh" means embodiment, or body: God becomes manifest as flesh, as form, as individuality. Let us see how the word "flesh" can be applied to a law of natural science such as gravity. The law of gravity was discovered when Isaac Newton observed that every time an object was dropped or permitted to fall into space, it gravitated toward the earth. His observation of this recurring phenomenon took form in consciousness—became flesh—and his subsequent deductions gave this law of nature a tangible body which became known as the law of gravity. The law of gravity had always had a body, because it had always existed as an operative law, but now Newton gave it another body, a body of knowledge. It now became embodied within consciousness.

In the same way, the laws of aerodynamics and electricity have always existed, and because they have always existed, they have form or flesh. They existed as the word—the invisible and unknown law, intangible, unwitnessed—until one day these laws took form in the human mind. Long before the first airplane flew or the first electric light bulb gave forth light, these laws were flesh, that is, they had taken on form as the principle of aerodynamics or the principle of electricity. All that was necessary was to externalize these principles in another form of flesh. As soon as the research scientist gained a knowledge of electricity and of electric light, these principles had form or body—a body of knowledge. Then, when the electrical engineer applied this knowledge, it became the form and body which we behold as electric lights and electrical devices. But you can see that it first had to have form and body in the mind of an Edison. So it is with art or music. It has form in the artist's or composer's consciousness—definite form and sound and beauty—then, outwardly, it has another form when it appears as printed notes of music, paintings, or sculpture. Do you see the difference here?

We are embodied in the mind of God as spiritual form. Then, we appear outwardly in some concept of form. That concept is changeable; that concept is destructible because it is finite. Those of you who can go back in memory to the early automobiles and compare them with the present-day modern motor vehicles can see how the outer form or concept changes, even though the principle of automotive engineering remains essentially the same. The principle is the same; the only thing that is different is its outer form. Does that help you to see the point we are making about the changeable nature of form?

Spiritually, the Word which is God, the Unmanifest, becomes manifest as the Christ, or Son of God, a manifested idea in consciousness. So Christ, the Son of God, is our invisible being, and this person, which you are, is its visible evidence. You and I, individually, are the visible, outward evidence of our invisible Christhood. We exist in the bosom of God as the Christ. We appear on earth as the son of man, but we are the selfsame Christ externalized as form, individuality.

This is the relationship between God and your infinite, eternal, individual being. God is your Selfhood. In the mind which is God, you are flesh, manifested, evidenced, witnessed. You are God, incarnate; you are form; you are individuality. Thus it is that all those, who have ever lived, who now live, and who will live, exist now in the flesh, in spiritual form and integrity, eternality, and immortality; and it is those of whom we read, "Yet in my flesh shall I see God,"[22] that is, in my spiritual consciousness, in spiritual individuality. "I will pour out my Spirit upon all flesh."[23] We, in our fleshly, spiritual identity, can know God; we can be as gods in that spiritual identity which we are; and we can think it not unseemly to do the works of God.

Flesh as Concept

Now we come to the word "flesh" as it is used in another sense in certain scriptural passages: "Flesh and blood cannot inherit the kingdom of God ..."[24] There shall no flesh be justified in his sight ..."[25] No flesh shall have peace."[26] In such citations, "flesh" can be translated into the word "concept." These earthly and human concepts will never be spiritual, and they will never reveal God. That body which is observed by the human senses is not body, but a universal concept of body. It has no existence except in the mind. The *body* is the Word made flesh, but in our present state of consciousness, most of us can see only a concept of body. This concept must die. Even the concept that you entertain of yourself must die because a concept can never know God. The concept you entertain of yourself as man, as effect—as sinful, sickly, and human—must die so that you become aware of this great truth: I am *that I am*, and *that* is what I am. When this realization comes, your old concept of yourself has died. You have fulfilled Paul's injunction to "die daily" and are being reborn of the Spirit. Yes, even the concept that you entertain of yourself must die because that concept can never know reality, can never know God. Only as you refrain from judging by appearances, only as you let God define *what* you are and *who* you are, only through a transformation of consciousness—"Be ye transformed by the renewing of your mind"[27]—will the answer come: "This is my beloved Son, in whom I am well pleased."[28] In reality, you are the beloved Son, the Word made flesh, but that flesh is an infinite individuality and an infinite body that is eternal:

"The word was made flesh"[29]—individually manifested as you and as me. It is the I which I am. Has anyone ever seen that

I with his eyes? Have I ever seen it? Have you ever seen it? No, you have never seen me, and I have never seen you. I have seen your body and I have seen my own body—my concept of body— but I have not seen you, and you have not seen me.

The I is invisible, perfect, complete, forever and forever. If any part of this form that I see is maimed or injured, I am just as complete, I am just as perfect, I am just as harmonious. That I of me is the Word made flesh. It is God individualized, God made tangible, God made evident. That I is intact, complete, and perfect now, and so it will be a thousand years from now—a million years from now. This I that I am is the unfolding of the I which is God, and is immaculately conceived. I am up here looking out of my eyes, invisible to the world. I am a state of Self-completeness in God, not self-complete as a human being, but, because God-being is my being, I am Self-complete. I embody within myself the fullness of the Godhead.

In this spiritual realization of your individual embodiment, you can truly say, "Yet in my flesh shall I see God."[30] Flesh, beheld through the senses, is our concept of our real identity; flesh, apprehended spiritually in meditation, is our spiritual form, not only of body, but of being. God, in individualizing Itself as your being and mine, has been made flesh, evident and tangible: The Word became flesh. That which you behold with the senses is the world's concept of flesh. That concept is changeable and must die. It will die, either through an acceptance of the world-belief of age, disease, and death, or by a transformation of consciousness. The decision lies with you. God has no pleasure in your dying. Turn ye and live. If you accept the world's concept of age and disease, that concept will know death, and nothing can save it. On the other hand, you can bring about the death of your concept of body painlessly by outgrowing it. As you realize more fully the nature of the Word made flesh, you drop the mortal concept of flesh and, ultimately, find your-self with a disease-less, ageless, and painless body. As you live in the conscious realization of God as the Source and creative Principle of your being and of your body, and "as you abide in me and my words abide in you," you will die to the flesh through transformation. The body will show forth an ever better appearance—youth, vitality, and strength. Outwardly, it will appear as an improved concept, but it will not be that—it will be your realization made manifest.

"For if ye live after the flesh ye shall die; but if ye through the Spirit do mortify the deeds of the body, ye shall live."[31] Use the word "consciousness" in place of "Spirit" and it reads: If ye, through your consciousness of truth do mortify the deeds of the body, ye shall live. In other words, if you live by that which has externalized form, that is, a concept, that concept will die. For instance, one who lives and depends solely upon money for his supply and upon material reliances for his well-being must eventually die, for this is the flesh that is as grass and all the glory of man as the flower of grass.

"He that soweth to his flesh shall of the flesh reap cor-ruption ... "[32] That sense of flesh is the earthly one. And how do you sow to the flesh? If you conduct your life as if this body were you and live your life catering to this body, you are sowing to the flesh and reaping corruption. If your attention is on your figure, your food, your health, or the type of automobile you drive, or whether or not your house is better than your neighbor's house, you are sowing to the flesh: You are concerned with the outward form. Neglecting your spiritual life, in a mad pursuit of the pleasures of sense, the profits of sense, or even the beauties of sense, is sowing to the flesh, and the reaping of corruption follows. There is nothing wrong about beautiful and gracious living when it comes as an added thing, as the effect of spiritual unfoldment. Enjoy all the good "flesh" of the world—the form—as long as it is an outer unfoldment of an inner grace. "Man shall not live by bread alone"—by reliance upon matter, by forms—"but by every word that proceedeth out of the mouth of God."[33]

In his great wisdom, the Master taught us that we need have no concern for that which has outer form:

> Lay not up for yourselves treasures upon earth, where moth and rust doth corrupt ... But lay up for yourselves treasures in heaven.[34]

> I am the bread of life: he that cometh to me shall never hunger; and he that believeth on me shall never thirst.[35]

> I have meat to eat that ye know not of.[36]

That bread, that meat, is the inner flesh that is in and of God.

"In my Father's house are many mansions,"[37] many states of consciousness, many embodied forms; and these states of consciousness will externalize themselves in what we call flesh, in infinite form and variety. Enjoy all good that comes to you, but do not cling to it or depend upon it. Be willing to see it come and be willing to see it go, always making room for greater unfoldment from within. The inner flesh is unchangeable, but it keeps externalizing itself in ever new, higher, and finer forms.

> Except a corn of wheat fall into the ground and die, it abideth alone: but if it die, it bringeth forth much fruit.[38]

A transformation is taking place in your consciousness, and it is breaking up the old patterns in order that the new life may come forth. This may be a painful process, but the pain comes because of wanting to cling to the old. You must be willing to undergo that transformation of consciousness, to let your old thought patterns and body forms go, that you may emerge into the flesh which is seen and understood as your real, eternal, and infinite individuality. This flesh will continuously externalize itself in newer and finer forms of body and bodily functions, which will be the visible manifestation of your higher state of consciousness.

Our work is not to get rid of the body, but rather to be clothed upon with a new concept of body. Sometime we shall all put off this outer envelope and step out into a higher heritage: "For we know that if our earthly house of this tabernacle were dissolved, we have a building of God, an house not made with hands, eternal in the heavens."[39] Some will die after the flesh, and some will voluntarily lay down this form for a higher one, that "mortality might be swallowed up of life."[40]

Let us remember, all cause is embodied in our own being. That cause is forever appearing as effect, and therefore, that effect must "die daily" in order that the new form may be born—may be formed, expressed, and revealed.

God is my being, my Selfhood, my consciousness; and this consciousness, which I am, is the law, the life, and the truth, appearing visibly as my daily experience. The body does not influence me: I influence the body. The body is not a law unto me: I am a law unto my body. The truth that I know is the law unto my being and my body. I am consciousness, and the consciousness, which I am, governs and controls the body: The body does not control consciousness; consciousness controls the body.

That is right identification.

ACROSS THE DESK

Across this desk comes mail from three-quarters of the globe and from the many states and stages of consciousness which constitute the world of truth-seekers. Most of those who write me are students seeking help with their personal problems: health, supply, and family, business, professional, and community relationships. Some seek help for friends or relatives, and even for problems of much wider scope.

Most of these people quickly understand that our work is not in the nature of giving human advice or counsel, and they are grateful that we inject no human evaluation or judgment into our work, but that whenever any problem whatsoever is brought to our consciousness, we go into meditation until His peace descends upon us and His Spirit is brought into activity in the situation or in the person. Thus there is *in our thought* no condemnation, no judgment, and no criticism. We are not in the position of attempting the healing, changing, or reforming of a human being, but rather of retiring into that state of consciousness, exemplified by Paul's statement that "neither circumcision availeth anything, nor uncircumcision ..."[41] Thus we are released from the picture presented, and from any idea of changing that picture; we find the deep well of contentment within, as the Spirit bears witness with our Spirit, and harmony appears, where discord had previously claimed existence.

Some students have already found themselves a part of The Infinite Way activity as practitioners, conductors of tape recording meetings, and even as instructors to beginners of the basic principles of our work. These workers often look to me for advice and guidance in their activities, and this I am happy to give. After twenty-eight years in the healing work, and ten years of continuous lecturing, teaching, and writing, such advice or counsel as it is my joy to give whenever, wherever, and by whomever requested should prove helpful.

It must be remembered, however, that all those who embark on any spiritual activity are strictly "on their own" with God. Each one must fail or succeed according to the

measure of his own developed state of consciousness. The
time must never come when it is necessary for me to say,
"If I go not away, the Comforter will not come unto you."[42]
Our Infinite Way writings are very clear, and the teaching
so direct and complete, that with the help given through
the Writings and Recordings, the lectures and class-work,
and my personal contact with students, or my contact with a
large number of them through correspondence, our students
must inevitably reach that point in consciousness where
they achieve contact with the Source of their own being,
God, and receive impartations of wisdom, love, guidance,
and direction, directly from the Source of all wisdom, the
Infinite Invisible. Until such time, students should not enter
into any public activity of a spiritual nature, although each
should respond to every call made upon him for spiritual
help. Every Infinite Way student has sufficient understanding and grace to turn within and give specific help to those
who seek such help from him.

In no way or at no point, do I seek to govern or control
the activity of any student. Each one who is engaged in the
work of The Infinite Way is responsible to God, alone, for his
activity. I have made but one request of students: Whenever
anyone or any group comes to you for help or instruction in
The Infinite Way, be certain that you are giving *only* that
which is presented by or in or as The Infinite Way. This is not
an attempt to limit the study, reading, or activity of anyone,
anywhere. It is an act of love to give those seeking The
Infinite Way teaching the purest Infinite Way you know.
When one or more desire some other teaching, instruction,
or help, release them. Set them free to go where that teaching, whatever its name or nature, can be given to them in the
purest way.

Our success is not measured by the number of students, patients, or so-called followers. Our success is measured by the amount or degree of our healing work and by the lives of students who are given freedom from the fears, doubts, limitations, dependencies, and even the pleasures of "this world." No organization must be permitted to creep into the activities of The Infinite Way beyond the unincorporated activity of providing an opportunity for study—no followers, no members, no possession of anyone, at any time.

Students of The Infinite Way are under no obligation to me at any time for anything. What I have done, or what I am doing or ever shall do, is for the purpose of establishing in consciousness the principles which constitute The Infinite Way. It is a work given me to do. The principles were given me in meditation; the demand to teach came from God, not from man. The money, the publishers, and the many who called me to them or who have served with me—all these came as gifts of God. No one owes me anything for this. I am but fulfilling my service to the One who entrusted me with the work and who is providing all the tools.

I hope that our students in this work will likewise feel that no one owes them the obligation of remaining with them, or of being in debt to them. What we do, let us do it as to God and be grateful that God's grace enables us to bless mankind. Having contacted the Father within, our working students have made their demonstration. If we are faithful to our highest understanding and remain humble enough to be continuously taught of God—and willing to accept counsel of those whose qualifications enable them to give it—then our realization of God will appear as every person or thing necessary to our unfoldment, and we shall not be dependent on "man, whose breath is in his nostrils." It is God's function to call to us, or draw to us, those we can help and those through whom the activity is carried on and who provide the means for its support. In all things, let us look to, and depend upon, the constant realization of God to fulfil Itself as our perfect experience.

God's grace will become evident on earth, in proportion as students of all spiritual teachers and teachings become more unselfed in their service. And with every breath of your body, bless these spiritual teachers and teachings through which the knowledge of spiritual power and spiritual living is reaching human consciousness. Just as the United States has Christian Science, Divine Science, and Unity, as well as numberless individual, independent spiritual teachers, so England has its Henry Thomas Hamblin and another galaxy of stars in the heavenly firmament. In Holland, Sweden, Germany, the Holy Lands, North, Central, and South Africa, India, Japan, Australia—wherever men lift their thought to God—are found spiritual teachers, uniting invisibly in God-consciousness and bringing to earth the era now being inaugurated in which force is outlawed and out-moded as a means of settling international problems. Those who have advanced sufficiently spiritually and who are no longer *using* God for personal gain—those who have reached up to the stars and beyond to make contact with the Father within—are bringing this era into manifestation.

You who now daily seek God for God alone—not for things or conditions or persons, but who want God for the love of God, for union with God—will usher in the next stage of unfoldment, which will witness a world in which all disease has been ruled out of human consciousness.

✽ 4 ✽

APRIL

RESURRECTION

IT IS SAID in Scripture that the last enemy that shall be overcome is death. The Master, Christ Jesus, proved this statement by raising the dead. "For I have no pleasure in the death of him that dieth ... wherefore turn yourselves, and live ye."[1] With such scriptural authority, you should realize that death need be no part of anyone's experience. Acceptance of a process which culminates in passing on is but the acceptance of a universal belief so tenacious that, according to the Master, it is the last enemy that will be overcome. That is probably true. It may take many, many generations before we come to that place in consciousness where we can say with assurance:

I need not die. I, my true identity, my God-identity, can raise up this temple every three years, every three days, every three months. I am continuously renewing this body. I, the Christ of God, the reality of man, am forever about the Father's business of sloughing off, rebirthing, renewing, restoring, and resurrecting this vehicle for my expression.

That *I*, the Christ, can never be revealed to mortal or material consciousness, but our realization of the Christ uplifts consciousness, until it is so spiritualized that it can behold the inner vision of eternality and immortality here and now.

Let us go back through the years to the resurrection of the Master. Why did only about five hundred people witness the risen Jesus? There were multitudes at the Crucifixion, but only about five hundred witnessed the bodily Resurrection. Why? When Jesus stepped out of the tomb, he walked out of it in the same form in which you and I will walk out of our tombs when, to human sense, we seem to pass on. Not one of us will ever remain in a tomb longer than three days, and most of us will never find ourselves in a tomb. We shall have arisen before the burial takes place. But only those with spiritual vision will be able to witness our resurrection.

You will be well on the road to achieving this spiritual perception, if you accept the fact that even when you are sitting face to face looking at a person and talking with him, you cannot see him. All that you can see is his body, his form; but you cannot see him, because he is way back of his eyes, looking out at you. Furthermore, he cannot see you, because you, also, are back of your eyes, looking out at him. You may be assured of this: If your body were lying on the floor, lifeless, you would still be there looking out at him because this "you" is not encased in a frame. The "you" of you is as external to your body as *I am*, and *I am* is God.

We are not form, nor are we in a form: The real identity of us animates our form. If the form were destroyed, we would immediately animate another one because that which is *I* can raise up a new temple three days from now, three hours from now, three minutes from now. There is no such thing as death for any individual. That which we call the death of the form is an experience that comes to us only because of a universal acceptance of birth, maturity, and death. As a matter of fact, our body does die; that is, our *concept* of body has died many times since we were born. There probably is not a drop of blood in us at this moment that was in us a year or two ago or a hair of our head that we had a few years ago.

Every part of us is being built and rebuilt, is dying and being reborn, just like the parts of a tree. The form of a tree is continually dying, but the life of the tree is continually raising up a new form. Every tree has a new form in its cycle of time. So do we have a new body—a new concept of body—whether it is every year, as some physicians say, or every three years as others say. There is no doubt but that many parts of this form, called the body, are dying moment by moment. Some of them, such as the nails or hair, we deliberately remove. Yet because the body dies and is renewed minute by minute, we are not even aware of this dying process or of the rebirthing of the body.

We could go on unto eternity watching our body die every year or two, and new blood, new skin, new bones, and new flesh being formed, and never experience the death process or what we term passing on; but when that day of living indefinitely in *this* life-experience comes, it will of necessity bring with it the realization that there is no such thing as old age. Simply living more years and carrying around a weak, infirm body for someone else to bathe, feed, or support is not proving immortality.

Transition as an Activity of Consciousness

Transition is not a physical thing. Transition is an act of consciousness which appears physically. To each of us there comes a time to cease being human beings, to cease living our human lives. That does not mean that we must die; it does not mean that we must pass on to attain our spiritual estate. There are those here who have passed from living a human life and are now living a spiritual life on earth, although, if you were to see them, you might not be aware of the transition they have undergone because their outward appearance is not unlike our own. But that is only the appearance: Actually, they have attained their Christhood.

The Master was an example of a human being who made the transition in consciousness while still living on earth. If you had seen the Master, you would undoubtedly have been one of those who said, "That is our neighbor, Mary's son," or "That is our neighbor, the carpenter." But if you were of Peter's state of consciousness, you would have known that you were not looking at a carpenter, but at the Christ. To anyone who asked who this man was, you would have responded: "This is not a carpenter; this is the Christ, the Son of God. He has already made the transition and is now living a Christ-life instead of a human life." If this had not been true, Jesus could not have made the demonstration of appearing to the five hundred who witnessed him after the Crucifixion. It was because he, himself, was no longer of the "grave" state of consciousness that he could make himself visible to those who were likewise above the "grave" state of consciousness.

When spiritual transition does take place, it will be evident in the change that takes place in your life. This change may find expression in a hundred different ways. For example, you may have an appetite for one kind of food today and find tomorrow that you cannot eat it. On the other hand, you may never have tasted certain kinds of food and yet tomorrow discover that they are the only kinds of food that you enjoy. That is not a matter of taste; that is a matter of consciousness appearing in physical form. In the same way, you may have enjoyed certain pleasures—pastimes, exercises, or games—which, in your spiritual elevation, you no longer find satisfying. That frequently happens with the habit of smoking, drinking, or card-playing—activities that to some human beings are normal, sometimes absolutely necessary—and yet, after the moment of that spiritual transition, these diversions no longer continue to be a source of pleasure. The whole nature has been transformed. This does not mean that there is anything evil about golf or tennis, or even any great evil in smoking or an occasional drink. It merely means that such things no longer satisfy the changed state of consciousness. Their indulgence was permissible for a certain state of consciousness, just as toys were our chief source of pleasure at one stage of our experience, but then became not only unnecessary later on, but even distasteful because we had outgrown that particular state of consciousness. Through this transition, we outgrow the mortal or material state of consciousness and no longer indulge the human appetites or the human fears or anxieties.

It is this transition which takes place in consciousness to which Paul referred when he enjoined us to "die daily" in order that we might be reborn of the Spirit. Every day that we consciously remove ourselves from under the law and acknowledge ourselves to be living under grace, every day that we do that and every hour of every day that we have a conscious realization that we are living on the Invisible and by the Invisible rather than by anything visible, we are dying daily; and then one day it happens that we die completely and are reborn of the Spirit. When that moment arrives, there is no longer a human reaction to life: Life, then, is lived on an entirely different plane. One is not subject to the laws of the world; one is in the world, but not of it.

To every man and woman in this present age and in the foreseeable future—even to those who have made the transition to a spiritual state of consciousness—there will probably be a transition from earthly sight. The world may call it death or passing on, but it will not come as the result of old age, disease, or accident. Those people who have made this spiritual transition will not experience the torture of endless years of disease, the tragedy of accidents, nor the infirmities of old age, but will walk on to their next experience quickly and painlessly. I am convinced that the day will come when we, in the world, will continue endlessly visible to each other, never ageing past the point of maturity. We shall stand forth in the fullness of our realized Christhood, maintaining the full vigor of maturity throughout all time.

Resurrection as the Transformation of Life

Resurrection is much more than lifting ourselves out of a tomb in order to walk the earth again. The Master has already made that demonstration for us. Even though to human sense we may appear to pass on, our resurrection is assured—in far less than three days. We shall never be entombed; we shall never be buried or cremated—that will never happen to us. The tomb is our own concept of body. As long as we think of ourselves as body, we shall be concerned about our body; but as soon as we realize that we are not our fingernails or hair, we shall begin to understand that we are not the rest of the body either, and then we will lose all undue concern for the body. We do not have to make the demonstration of resurrection; it has already been made for us, and even our making it will not convince anybody on earth, unless some spiritually illumined person, seeing our demonstration of it, is given an added proof of its certainty.

But if we can prove resurrection here and now, if we can prove that our body—our concept of body—dies every year, as is indicated by the dropping of nails, hair, and skin, and probably, unseen to our eyes, muscle, flesh, and bones; and that, along with this process, our body is renewed year by year, so that we continue living on in youth, vitality, strength, and in the fullness of maturity—in the fullness of mental faculties and in the fullness of harmony—then, we shall be showing forth a resurrection which may awaken the world.

We have seen examples of that resurrection in the lives of many metaphysical and spiritual workers who have been active in their eighties and nineties, showing forth the full vigor of manhood and womanhood. This has been true of other people as well. There are islands in the South Pacific where people live in perfect and complete health until eighty, ninety, or a hundred and then one night quietly go to sleep and do not wake up in the morning. They have not died; they have completed their function on earth and they walk on just as the worm becomes the butterfly. But if the worm becomes the butterfly, do you doubt that a butterfly becomes something else? The evolution of life is just that. We shall not stay here in this form for eternity, but the nearer we get to our spiritual center, the nearer we will come to the demonstration of the Master's words: "Destroy this temple, and in three days I will raise it up"[1]—I can lay down my life and I can pick it up again.

At our present stage of unfoldment, there comes a call to each one of us, at some time or other, to leave this plane of existence. There seems to be no purpose in our remaining on earth visible to human sight indefinitely. At this stage of unfoldment, we are still dealing with time and space, with a world limited to a circumference of twenty-five thousand miles. Eventually, however, we shall discover the infinity of the universe, and with that discovery will come the realization that it is of no consequence whether we are visible or invisible to the world. That, you can only begin to recognize as you look in a mirror and realize that you are not standing there in form, but that you are looking out at yourself from behind your eyes, and that the "you" of you is not occupying space. As a matter of fact, you will learn one day that that "you" is I, that that "you" is all of us, that all of us really are not all of us at all, but only one of us, and that One is God. Then you will understand why it will not be necessary for anyone to pass from here to there, visible or invisible.

It takes spiritual apprehension to discern the *I* that I am because that *I* is invisible. Remember, everything that takes place must take place as an activity of consciousness. Nothing can happen out there. Everything is the effect of an activity of consciousness. When you have the consciousness of truth, your demonstration out here in the world is truth; when you have the consciousness of resurrection, your demonstration in the world is resurrection. As an individual comes to a realization of this truth, the harmonies of life begin to appear. The activity of truth in consciousness is the word of God made flesh as harmonious being. This activity of truth performs its holy work of revealing pure spiritual being.

The Spiritual Path

When a practitioner on the spiritual path is asked for help and he sits in silence and quietness waiting for the inflow of the Spirit, it is very often given to him to behold the spiritual identity, the spiritual entity of his patient, actually to see his patient as he is in God's image and likeness. If the practitioner rises high enough, he will catch glimpses of the real body, and that body is not a physical form, nor is it a male or female form, but yet it is form. It is as tangible as that which we see with the eye, only we are seeing it with the Soul and we are seeing it as it is. It is as if someone had sufficient vision to look out and see the sky from up in the sky, and the house from down on the ground, and at the same time all the space between. Our limited sense of vision does not permit that. So likewise, it is only in periods of enlightenment that our Soul-vision permits us to see the divine form, or this physical or bodily form as it really is. We are told that when we behold Him as He is, we shall be satisfied with that likeness. Yes, and when we see each other through our Soul-sense, then we shall be well satisfied with each other.

That is what takes place in healing. That is what brings about the healing. When one spiritually enlightened individual beholds reality, every form of discord or distress in range of that consciousness disappears. It is that which constitutes healing: the attainment on the part of one individual of even one single second of reality. In that second, the healing takes place.

When a teacher has a great deal of meditation work with students, in many cases, the teacher finally comes to an actual apprehension of the true identity of the student, and this awakens him out of his dormant state of humanhood into spiritual realization. The spiritually illumined teacher, being present with the student and meditating with him over a number of years, finally reaches right through the layers of humanhood to the center of that student's being and, through his own illumined consciousness, beholds the Son of God and awakens the student to his spiritual realization.

Whenever I have the opportunity of working with students over a number of years—not that it always takes years—eventually the two become one. The consciousness of the teacher beholds the consciousness of the student and awakens it. From that moment on, the student is free in his own spiritual light, consciously one with God, no longer needing teacher or teaching, since now he is able to receive impartations directly from the Spirit.

In our present state of spiritual ignorance, these experiences are rare. In the first place, there are not many Occidental teachers who have achieved that conscious union with God which makes this experience possible. In days to come, there will be more such teachers. The small number of qualified teachers, however, is matched by the few students sufficiently desirous of the God-experience and wanting that experience enough to be willing to dedicate their lives to achieving it. It is not something that comes in such off moments as our spare time will permit, nor can it be achieved with our spare change. It requires devotion, whole-hearted devotion, not for any human reason—because there is no personal benefit to be gained. As a matter of fact, the exact opposite takes place: In gaining this experience, the student loses the world. The way is straight and narrow and few there be that enter.

There are not many who realize that there is a spiritual kingdom called "My kingdom," that there is a peace that has nothing to do with any amount of money or any amount of honor or any amount of grandchildren or any amount of anything else that can be found in this world—a peace that transcends anything known to human sense. The few students of the Occident who have realized that such an experience is possible have embarked on the search for God-realization. Nothing will prevent their success, because they have reached the stage where nothing less than the God-experience, itself, will satisfy them.

The way is straight and narrow, but the way is not to disregard our duties or family responsibilities. Instead, it is to come into such spiritual demonstration that these responsibilities take their proper place, fall into line, making everything necessary for the achievement of the goal possible. It means praying so seriously and with such consecration, that the Spirit within opens out a pathway for the aspirant to find his teacher or his teaching, wherever these may be.

To many people coming into metaphysics, it is enough that metaphysical or spiritual help will take away the ills and the sins of the flesh or the limitations of the purse. Most people, therefore, rest on that rung of the ladder. In such human betterment, they have achieved their heart's desire: The disease is gone; the lack is gone; the unhappiness is gone; and now they can begin to enjoy life—"this world" life, the peace and satisfaction "this world" can give. There are some students, however, who are not satisfied with achieving the kind of peace that most men understand and desire, but they seek rather the peace that *passeth* understanding—the peace that this world can never give, regardless of how harmonious it is. There are those who are satisfied to find a law, if necessary a law of matter or a law of mind or a law of Spirit that will overcome the ills of the flesh. But there are others who could never rest until they come under grace; there, law cannot operate.

Resurrection: the Goal of the Spiritual Path

Such is the spiritual path. Its goal is resurrection and ascension. Resurrection from a tomb to walk the earth will prove little or nothing to anyone. To you who have set your foot upon the spiritual path, behold the resurrection: Recognize the Christ seated behind the eyes of every

individual, sitting in the heart of every individual, constitut-
ing the soul of every individual. Look through the physical
appearance of men and women to the *I* that sits back of their
eyes, looking out at you. Look through their claims of sin,
disease, lack, limitation, color, and religion to the Presence,
and, in so doing, you will have the actual experience of witnessing resurrection.

As you practice looking through the appearance to the
invisible Presence, you will have the same opportunity that
Jesus presented two thousand years ago to his followers. For
those of you who have eyes to see and ears to hear, "Destroy
this temple, and in three days I will raise it up."[2] Jesus gave
his followers the opportunity to see him, and the Christ
today will give you the same opportunity to witness the resurrection. At first, it may be the resurrection into sainthood
of someone whom you call a sinner. It may be the resurrection of a dying person, lifted up into spiritual health, because
you must remember that this spiritual path of ours in this
age is filled mostly with those who were sinners or who were
numbered among the living dead. Almost all of our effective
practitioners have been either at death's door, very sick, very
sinful, or very poor. They are bearing witness to resurrection
from some very low states of humanhood—virtually dead
states of humanhood.

As a matter of fact, if you were to investigate the history
of the practitioners and teachers who are really known for
their good healing work, who are known for living spiritual
lives, you will usually find that these people have been at
death's door either physically, morally, or financially, and
have been raised up by this power of the Spirit, so lifted up
into newness of life that now, when you look at them, you
are seeing what the world calls saints. They were not always

that way. They were dead in sin, or dead in disease, or dead in poverty, but now they are alive again in Spirit. It is possible that you may witness this form of resurrection before you witness the other form, that is, before you witness the raising up of those who have passed on.

The Teacher Within

Spiritual teaching is an impartation from an enlightened consciousness to a receptive consciousness. A student on the spiritual path receives truth from a teacher when the student sits silently listening, but when the student is permitted to argue, debate, or discuss truth, the whole situation is on the human level—on the intellectual plane—and no spiritual teaching takes place. If a student must hear the spoken word, let him go to his practitioner or teacher, listen, and sit in silent receptivity. The attitude in spiritual teaching is that the teacher is, at that moment, the master; the student is the student. Spiritual teaching can only take place through the impartation of the Word to the receptive thought. No student, who is a true student, will ever believe that he knows enough to discuss truth with a teacher; no teacher will ever believe that truth can be learned by discussion. That does not bar the student from asking questions, but it means that when a question is asked, even though the student may not be convinced, he is at least satisfied that the best answer available at the moment has been given.

When going into meditation, remember that your teacher is within you. Your teacher is enthroned within your consciousness. This teacher, you can meet face to face within your own being. Your teacher—the teacher within you—will never leave you nor forsake you; your teacher will never abandon you nor be absent from you—not even in the valley of the shadow of death, not even if you make your bed in hell, not even if you are in the depths of sin. Your teacher will never leave you, and you are at liberty any second to turn within, talk to your teacher as if your teacher were sitting in front of you, and eventually, you will learn to receive answers from your teacher. "*I* will never leave thee, nor forsake thee ...[3] *I* am with you alway, even unto the end of the world."[4] That is your teacher, the only teacher worth listening to, the true teacher. This teacher will lead you in the way everlasting.

> And thine ears shall hear a word behind thee, saying, This is the way, walk ye in it, when ye turn to the right hand, and when ye turn to the left ...[5] Arise, shine: for thy light is come, and the glory of the Lord is risen upon thee.[6]

ACROSS THE DESK

The observance of Easter commemorates the attained spiritual consciousness of the Master, and rightly understood, in our lives of contemplation, this holy day cannot be separated from Christmas, at which time the birth of the Master is commemorated. From birth to the Ascension, the Master's life is a continuous record of spiritual consciousness unfolding, disclosing, and revealing itself.

Christmas brings the promise of peace on earth to men of good will. In the life and teaching of the Master, we are shown the way to this gift of peace.

Heretofore, the world has considered much of the Master's teaching too impractical to be incorporated into everyday life. Now, with the world-wide spread of spiritual teachings like The Infinite Way, the world is better prepared for the acceptance of the truth which will actually set men free. In the following newspaper editorial, one of the editors of *The Dayton Journal Herald* plainly has in mind a major principle of The Infinite Way, that of praying for our enemies, as taught by the Master. This, of course, follows his startling teaching, "But I say unto you, That ye resist not evil. ..."

Christmas Peace

How beautiful the Christmas season is! Man has poured devotion on it, not only the devotion of a few days or months, but that of centuries.

Into Christmas observance he has brought customs from religions other than that of Christianity—the use of mistletoe and holly, the use of decorated tree. People of many lands have brought, to Christmas, carols and anthems. These we sing in our homes and in churches.

We listen again to the Bethlehem story and picture to ourselves a scene of shepherds as they hear sung from the skies: "On earth peace, good will toward men."[7]

It is at this point that some of us may wonder why, if peace be the gift of God, we have not received it. But, as we query this, would it not be well if we considered whether or not we have something to do that the peace of heaven be fulfilled in us. Have we steadfastly endeavored to put into practice the teachings of Jesus of Nazareth? Have we learned to forgive "seventy times seven" or to pray for our enemies?

True, we may believe these are instructions fit only for Sunday. And never, surely, have they been put into practice on a large scale. We have opened our churches during war-time to beseech blessings for our own soldiers, forgetting that the Master said that praying for our own avails little.

What if we should open our places of worship to pray for our enemies? Not, of course, that they be enabled to fulfil their human greeds, but rather that the center of their beings be opened so that, as the poet Browning says, "the imprisoned splendour may escape."

Then it could be that weapons would fall from our respective hands as we reached them out in a gesture of brotherhood, and enduring treaties be signed at the peace tables of the world. Then it could be that across the skies of the nations would sound the Christmas blessing: "On earth peace, good will to men."

In the spiritual journey from Christmas to Easter, the lesson is a continuous message of non-resistance to evil, of praying for those who in any way offend us, and of forgiving, forgiving, and forgiving. This reaches its height when the Master, before the Crucifixion, is taken prisoner and rebukes Peter who would defend and protect him, reiterating once again the two laws which were soon to carry the triumphant Master to full realization: "Put up again thy sword ... for all they that take the sword shall perish with the sword ...[8] Father, forgive them; for they know not what they do."[9]

Easter reveals the achievement of full Christhood by the Master and reveals the way by which we can attain immortality. The Christ-experience we seek is revealed from Christmas to Easter, and each step must be taken in its proper order to enable us to achieve the ascension above material sense. And here let each student remember that we are called upon to rise above the so-called good material sense as well as the erroneous. The Christ-experience leads to the ascension above the human mode of life to the spiritual.

This season of the year is a good time in which to review our program on the path of The Infinite Way. Herewith is a summary of steps to be taken on our journey from Christmas to Easter:

The Infinite Way Reveals

I. The nature of the Christ-experience

    A. A present possibility

    B. When achieved, the Christ takes over our experience

    C. The Christ acts as a power performing that which is our work

    D. The Christ draws to us everything necessary to our daily life

1. Persons
2. Things
3. Supply
4. Opportunity
5. Activity
6. Reward
7. Recognition

II. The nature of God, correcting the false impressions of current teachings

III. The nature of the Christ-mission, now and of old, correcting prevalent beliefs

IV. The nature of prayer according to the revelation of Jesus Christ

A. Receptivity to the Word which is uttered or expressed *to* you from *within* you

B. Prayer is the word of God

1. Not something a person speaks or thinks
2. That which God utters and we hear, receive, or become aware of—"he uttered his voice, the earth melted"[10]

V. The nature of spiritual meditation leading to communion and union

VI. The nature of individual being

A. "I and my Father are one"[11]

B. God constitutes individual being

1. I have all that the Father hath
   a. Infinity
   b. Allness
   c. Supply
   d. Home
   e. Companionship
2. Nothing can be added to individual being
   a. Through Christ, I can do all things
   b. Through my Christhood, I am and have all things

   c. I have meat, wine, water

   d. Instead of drawing to me, I live out from the center

VII. The nature of the healing and saving power

 A. Healing is not the result of conscious thinking, but of ideas imparted to consciousness from within

 B. God is

   1. Perfection is—completeness, harmony, health, joy

   2. We must bring ourselves into this perfect state of being

    a. Acknowledge him in all thy ways

    b. "Thou wilt keep him in perfect peace, whose mind is stayed on thee"[12]

    c. "Abide in me, and I in you"[13]

 C. Healing does not improve the mortal man, but reveals the Christ-man as individual you and me

VIII. The nature of error

 A. Understanding the nature of that which appears as error

 B. Knowing neither good nor evil

IX. Truth revealed

 A. By being consciously known, read, and declared

 B. Through receptivity, Truth is imparted from within

It is now mid-February and out here in Hawaii, the rains and winds of winter are giving way to longer days of warm sunshine. At Lotus Garden, twenty of us have completed two weeks of advanced class work—The Kailua Advanced Class. Suddenly, one night the call came to conduct this work, and within three days, a group of twenty had assembled and were ready for it. It is an advanced class. Everyone can benefit from it in some measure and will find the tapes on which it is recorded of value, but only those who have studied The Infinite Way earnestly for some time will have the developed consciousness to absorb it.

This class had its beginning in New York City, March, 1956, and was continued in Melbourne, Australia; Chicago, Illinois; Seattle, Washington; Portland, Oregon; Victoria and Vancouver, Canada; New York City, November, 1956; and finally the circle was completed in *The Kailua Advanced Class* in Hawaii. This last Kailua Class embraces the highlights of the 1956 work, plus the fruitage of our three daily sessions of healing work. Recordings of this class are being studied in Australia, Africa, Canada, England, and the United States.

Those of you who have followed the monthly *Letter* and have heeded my advice in regard to the study of the message of The Infinite Way will now be prepared to take a higher step in spiritual unfoldment. This is the work leading us through the transitional stages into the spirit of truth. Here students practice the surrender of the use of the letter of truth so that life may be lived by grace. Those who attempt this step before thoroughly understanding the letter of Truth cannot hope to succeed, but those students who have been patient in learning and practicing with the letter can now experience the actual consciousness or spirit of truth.

Those individuals who continue as students of The Infinite Way will require even greater patience and perseverance as we now take up the work of higher spiritual consciousness. Here our concern is not merely exchanging inharmonious physical, mental, moral, or financial conditions for harmonious ones, but rising now above the harmonious conditions of human life into the spiritual. Heretofore, students have understood metaphysical and spiritual study as a means of bringing the activity of the Christ to conscious experience to dispel the discords of sense. Now they will realize that the activity of the Christ, realized, dispels *all* material sense—the good as well as the evil material or human conditions—and reveals spiritual harmony, spiritual activity, spiritual grace. As a foundation for this higher atmosphere of life, an even deeper study of the Writings and Recordings, more meditation, and greater healing work will now be required of those who have been on The Infinite Way with us during these years.

In this higher consciousness, you will begin—slowly perhaps—to experience *My* peace, *My* meat, wine, water, *My* life, and *My* joy. In this consciousness, you experience the kingdom of God and His strength, His power, His wisdom. This is the Fourth Dimension of Life. It is the goal of Infinite Way living.

About the middle of March, I expect to leave Hawaii to spend a few days in Chicago and New York, *en route* to London, where I shall spend the month of April giving lectures and conducting classes. Following this, there will be two weeks on the Continent before I return to my new home in Hawaii. By the time you receive this *Letter*, I shall be in Europe taking this message to Edinburgh, Scotland; Manchester, Blackpool, and London, England; The Hague, Holland; Germany; and Switzerland.

With three dedicated Infinite Way students, I have been working all month on healing work—several sessions each day and evening—and through this effort, we hope to show forth greater works and make healing more simple for our students to achieve and practice.

In the monthly *Letter*, the younger students will find the steps necessary for their instruction and practice, and the advanced student, before reading and studying *The Letter*, will find, through earnest prayer, the higher steps and the spiritual atmosphere necessary to progressive spiritual unfoldment and God-realization.

✤ 5 ✤

<u>MAY</u>

THE CHRIST, THE PRESENCE IN YOU

THERE IS A PRESENCE and a Power which is always available to us, but it can only be realized in secrecy and in silence. Secrecy is one of the most profound truths revealed in the Master's teaching:

> Take heed that ye do not your alms before men, to be seen of them: otherwise ye have no reward of your Father which is in heaven.
>
> Therefore when thou doest thine alms, do not sound a trumpet before thee, as the hypocrites do in the synagogues and in the streets, that they may have glory of men. Verily I say unto you, They have their reward.
>
> But when thou doest alms, let not thy left hand know what thy right hand doeth:
>
> That thine alms may be in secret: and thy Father which seeth in secret himself shall reward thee openly.
>
> And when thou prayest, thou shalt not be as the hypocrites are: for they love to pray standing in the synagogues and in the corners of the streets, that they may be seen of men. Verily I say unto you, They have their reward.[1]

Secrecy is an important principle of The Infinite Way and forms a vital part of its message. Those who have taken this teaching seriously and have followed it have benefited beyond words. There are others who have received the teaching, but who have not understood it. In their inability to perceive its significance, they have not obeyed it, and therefore, have not benefited from it.

No teaching is of real value as long as it remains an abstraction; it must find expression in our daily life. Every principle of The Infinite Way should be related to our experience and then lived as our experience. Let us take, as an example, this principle of secrecy enunciated by the Master and see how it can be applied to our everyday relationships.

If I perform some good and generous act and if my friends hear about it, they will, in all probability, praise me, thank me, and speak well of me. My ego may be considerably inflated by their acknowledgment and recognition of my good deed. On the other hand, if I do some good deed, but keep it secret, so well-locked up within myself that no man knows about it, the all-seeing Eye and the all-knowing Mind, this omnipresent, infinite Intelligence, that knows all about what I have done, witnesses my good works in secret and then, in some mysterious way that It has, rewards me openly.

In the same way, if I pray publicly with sufficient noise and ostentation, the newspapers and magazines may write articles about my praying seven or seventy times a day, and I am sure that there will be some men and women who will puff me up with their adulation. But of what benefit is that? If, however, I pray in secret, if I commune with the Father within me, the Father, which is omnipresence, omniscience, divine intelligence, and divine love, knows that I am praying, and I am rewarded, not by man, but by God.

This principle of maintaining the sacredness and integrity of our spiritual life by keeping secret every thought and deed motivated by the Spirit operates in all fields of life. It is especially fruitful when applied to our relationships with each other. There is only one way to love your neighbor as yourself, and that is to love him in the same way in which you love yourself. Humanly, you know your own faults, your own weaknesses; and humanly, you may criticize yourself severely because you know that you do not measure up to your own highest standard of what is right. Yet, in spite of all that, inwardly, you know that the Christ is your true identity and that you are spiritual, even when you fail to live up to that high ideal. Actually, you are the child of God, spiritual and perfect, and every day you pray that your outer actions will conform to that which you know about your inner Self. The only way you can love yourself is by knowing your true identity as the child of God.

Recognize the Christ in All Men

To love your neighbor as yourself, you must do the same for him that you do for yourself. Realize that in spite of his human faults and failings, your neighbor is the same Son of God that you are—but do not stop with knowing this about your neighbor. This is true, not only of your neighbor, but of every person you meet. It is true even of your enemy—personal, national, racial, or religious. In the secret place of your inner being, know that the Christ sits enthroned in the heart and soul and mind and body of every individual on earth.

When you talk to your employer or employee, when you meet tradespeople, or when you see friends or relatives, inwardly greet every one of them: "Greetings, child of God. I salute in you the Christ of God." Say it silently and secretly. Do not let anyone know that you are doing this. Let the results speak for themselves. Never doubt, for a moment, that all those whom you meet will quickly discover something in you that changes their whole attitude toward you, although they, themselves, may not know what it is. Eventually, you will hear them say, "You have something. What is it?" Of course, what you have, and what they are feeling, and the thing to which they are responding is the knowledge of their true identity and your willingness to acknowledge it in spite of appearances to the contrary. This recognition of the Christ in the secrecy of your own being is rewarded openly.

We are apt to wonder why people, sometimes even our own associates, are not more friendly to us than they are. But the reason is very plain: We are holding them in condemnation to their humanhood. It is unfortunate enough that they are doing this to themselves without increasing their burden by adding our own condemnation to their already severe judgment of themselves. Release them; set everyone free by beholding the Son of God in every person you meet.

In this work there is a continual aloneness, but it is never lonesomeness. There is an aloneness, the aloneness of an individual's being one with God, but separate from the rest of the world. But in such oneness with God, there is no such thing as being lonely because there is a tabernacling with this It, with this Presence, this Spirit, that sometimes you can even feel moving around in you. In your experience, there will always be people present to express love and understanding—more than you have title opportunity to enjoy fully—but the aloneness remains.

The Master's principle of secrecy is very powerful. You do not have to leave your home to attract your good to you, whether it be in the form of friends or opportunity. You can sit quietly in your home, in your place of business, or in your church, temple, or class and you can draw the world to yourself. But it can be done only through God, and not through man. Business firms advertise and frequently divert a large portion of their budget to this purpose in an attempt to double or redouble their business. You will discover, however, that you can draw your good to you without the expenditure of large sums of money. Take the few dollars, or even the few cents which you may have, and share them with someone secretly, so that the rest of the world does not know that you have shared them. It does not have to be money: Share books, service, or share a prayer, but share something which only God knows about and be sure that you tell no man what you have done. You will find that what God sees in secret, He first multiplies tenfold or a hundredfold and then shows it forth so unmistakably that all men can see it.

Your heavenly Father is within you. Is it not fantastic to believe that you could do anything that would not be known to the heavenly Father? Whatever God witnesses in secret is rewarded outwardly in our affairs. This principle works in the living of our lives on this human plane, but it brings with it spiritual fruitage. Let us learn to acknowledge secretly that we are the children of God, that regardless of our human failings, the Christ sits enthroned in our innermost being; and then, let us remember to acknowledge that same truth for our neighbor, whether that neighbor be friend or foe, associate or competitor. Let us recognize Christ as individual being, but let us do it secretly, silently, sacredly, and watch the magic that takes place in our lives. There is no secret about how to make friends. Recognize the spiritual identity of every person you meet and you will soon have more friends than you could possibly want or need.

Realize the Christ Around the World

Through transportation by jet propulsion in this atomic age, distances have been reduced almost to the zero point. The distance that once took months to travel can now be bridged in a few hours. The whole world has become our neighborhood, and people living thousands of miles away from us, our neighbors. It is not enough to number our friends by their immediate proximity to us on the same street or in the same neighborhood. We must extend our concept of friend and neighbor so that it becomes broad enough to include the world. Inclusiveness, rather than exclusiveness, must be our goal. This necessitates the relinquishment of the bigotries and the dogmatism which would separate and divide one man from another. We are all conditioned by prenatal influences, home environment, education, and personal experiences, and because of those influences and experiences, we interpret other ways of life in terms of our own background. That is what makes us human beings. Try as we will, there is no way by which we can give up these preconceived ideas—except one. When Spirit touches consciousness, all previous concepts disappear, regardless of their tenacity. Then, we no longer hug to ourselves our Protestantism, Judaism, or Catholicism, our racial pride, or our economic sufficiency or insufficiency. Now, these things take their proper place, and we are one with all life, one in the realization, not only of our own identity, but in the recognition of the true identity of every person and thing.

Only the touch of the Spirit—the Presence within—can transform consciousness so that our lives show forth more love, more generosity, more freedom, more justice, mercy, equity, and more gentleness and peace. Memorizing words in a book will not do this for us. There are people who have memorized whole books of truth-teaching, and nothing has happened. There has been no change in their lives. They have added more knowledge to an already heterogeneous mass of undigested statements about God and the universe, but such knowledge has not touched their Soul. Knowledge, alone, cannot touch the Soul, because the word of God is not the word of God when it comes out of the human mind. Only a conscious realization of the presence of God, a realization of the Christ, can unite us in true brotherhood and lasting friendship and dissolve the mesmeric sense which binds us in chains to "me," "mine," and "thine."

The activity of the Christ can never be limited to operating exclusively for our own selfish purposes or for those of our families. The purpose of the Christ is to establish the kingdom of God on earth—not to bring good to a few favored individuals who know the right words. I am convinced that the world can be transformed through the realization of the Christ in individual consciousness. Many years ago, I envisioned a band of Christ-consciousness around the world, having no human ties of any kind, but dedicated to a conscious realization of the presence of the Christ on earth as in heaven:

> Illumination dissolves all material ties and binds men together with the golden chains of spiritual understanding; it acknowledges only the leadership of the Christ; it has no ritual or rule but the divine, impersonal universal Love; no other worship than the inner Flame that is ever lit at the shrine of Spirit. This union is the free state of spiritual brotherhood. The only restraint is the discipline of the Soul, therefore we know liberty without license; we are a united universe without physical limits; a divine service to God without ceremony or creed. The illumined walk without fear—by Grace.[2]

Anyone can be a part of that invisible band who is willing to sit in silence until he has a conscious feeling that God is on the field—that all is well. When that feeling comes, he has released the Christ into the world, this Christ that has been locked up inside of his heart. The Christ realized dissolves the errors of this world which we may lump together in one term, material sense. The realized Christ operates in human consciousness, making it receptive to Truth. Little by little, the Christ is taking hold of human consciousness, but the Christ can only come to consciousness through realization. The Christ is always there and has always been there, but it is only in the degree of our realization of It that It becomes active in our experience:

Somewhere within me there is a Presence. It eludes description, but it is a Presence which I can feel and of which I am aware most of the time. It is always present, but there are times, after a busy day or night, when I may not feel It and be able consciously to touch It or be touched by It. Then, at such times, I become very still and quiet, and suddenly It returns to my conscious awareness.

This Presence performs whatever work is done through me. I am not the worker; I am the instrument for Its activity. It is this Presence which does the work through me or does it for me. If I sit quietly with an inner receptivity, It prays; It utters that voice which makes the earth melt; It meditates. I merely become silent, while It performs Its work in me and through me. Christ, the Son of God, lives my life. I can of mine own self do nothing. If I speak of myself, I bear witness to a lie. It is this Presence within me that is my capacity and my talent, and it is this It which is performing Its function through me.

Christhood reigns in me. Christhood flows through me to this world. Christhood animates my every act. Christhood flows through me to bless every individual with whom I come in contact. Christhood is the measure and the capacity of my experience.

This Presence, this Christ or Son of God, is within each one of us, performing for us and as us. However, It functions only for the person who has achieved Its realization. You are only the Son of God when the Spirit of God worketh in you. You are not the Son of God while you are using the personal sense of "I." You are a selfhood cut off, in belief, from

God, entertaining a sense of separation from God. When you begin to see that the good you do is not being done by you, you may be able to break through Paul's dilemma, "The good that I would I do not: but the evil which I would not, that I do."[3] At that stage of Paul's development, there was an "I," but that was no longer true when he could say, "I live, yet not I, but Christ liveth in me."[4] In his earlier stage, he had to admit, as do we, "I am better inside than I am outside. I would love to be doing good things, but I am always doing the wrong ones, or nearly always." That is true of us only when we are in the state of "I."

Divine Adequacy

When, through meditation—and this Presence is only realized through meditation—you finally come face to face with the fact that there is an inner Selfhood, an inner you, then "greater is he that is in you, than he that is in the world."[5]

This He *that is within me is my true being; It is my spiritual Selfhood; It is the Christ which overshadows me, the Spirit of God in me, Immanuel or God with me.*

As you acknowledge that and step a little bit aside from yourself to let It have sway, you become aware that many things are done through you and by you, which inwardly you know that you consciously did not do and consciously could not have known how to do. *It* did them through you.

Many times you have undoubtedly entertained a sense of limitation about your own capacity. You may feel, whether it is in the healing work or whether it is in the field of business, in some professional activity, or in your relationship with relatives, friends, or associates, that you are inadequate, and no doubt you are and always will be. The more you become aware of the Presence, the more will you realize your own inadequacy as a human being, until eventually you know, as did Jesus, "I can of mine own self do nothing."[6] When that realization comes, you will be performing wonders in your own field of endeavor, but you will know it is not you who are doing it; you will know that It is doing the work.

Every one of us has this It within him. Every one of us has the Spirit of God, or the Christ, at the center of his being, but most of us have not come fully into the conscious awareness of It, or else that awareness has been felt only once in a great while. We have not yet reached the stage where we can achieve it as a matter of will, or where we live in it all the time. The day comes, however, when this Withinness, this inner Self, is functioning all the time, and most of the time we are consciously aware of It, and on the few occasions when we are not, we can restore ourselves to Its awareness by deeper meditation. It is always present, awaiting our recognition. By It, we can do all things.

Acknowledge that there is a He within you and that this He is greater than any circumstance or condition in the world. Then, having recognized that, begin to practice acknowledging It in every circumstance of life. In the beginning, you may have no feeling at all of the Presence. In that event, you may have to accept the word of the Hebrew prophets, of the Christian mystics, or of the Asian mystics, all of whom have found it to be true that there is a He or a Me within. "Look unto me, and be ye saved[7] ... Is there any God beside me?" says Isaiah, "I know not any."[8] In the Bhagavad Gita, there are whole passages that caution us never to seek for things, but to seek only Me, recognize only Me in the midst of you; acknowledge Me in the midst of you. Innumerable passages of Hebrew and Christian Scripture reveal the fact that there is a He, a Christ, a Father, a Spirit of God in us. With such impressive authority, be willing, even if you do not experience it at once, at least to acknowledge that these men were wise and truthful, and that their lives and the lives of their disciples bear witness to the fact that this is true.

The same He that was within Christ Jesus is within you, and, furthermore, It has the same power in you that It had in Christ Jesus. The same power which raised up spiritual truth in one era, raises it up in another. That same power which was the God of Abraham, Isaac, and Jacob, that same power which was the Spirit that raised up Jesus Christ from the dead, that opened the Red Sea for Moses, that made manna fall from the sky, that same Power which carried Paul through persecutions, that same Power dwells in you. All of these great spiritual lights have revealed that He that is within you is greater than any circumstance, person, or condition in the world. He that is within you performeth whatever it is that is appointed for you to do. He that is within you perfecteth that which concerneth you. This He is closer than breathing and nearer than hands or feet:

Before Abraham was, I am with you. I will never leave you nor forsake you. I will be with you unto the end of the world. If you walk through the waters, I will go with you; if you go through the flames, I will go through them with you.

There is a Presence within you, and Its name is I. First, recognize this Presence and then begin the daily and hourly acknowledgment of It. If necessary, every hour on the hour, acknowledge:

I, in the midst of me, is mighty. I, in the midst of me, was with me since before Abraham was and will be with me unto the end of the world. If I go through the valley of the shadow of death, I will go with me. Wherever I go, I will go with me; whether it is up in an airplane, down in a submarine, or wherever it may be, I *am always in the midst of me. This* I *performeth the work that is given me to do.*

The day will come when you will realize that you have done and are doing things that you, of yourself, did not have the capacity to do: *I* did them through you—the *I* of your own being, that It, which we call the Christ, did these things. Recognizing and understanding *I* as the doer, you can receive appreciation, but never will you take praise or consider money as your personal possession. Once you understand that what you are receiving is for something that *I*, the Spirit of God within you, have done through you, you will always consecrate it to the purpose of the *I*, the spiritual message and mission.

Acknowledge Him in All Thy Ways

"I live, yet not I."[9] Christ performeth that which is given me to do. This is the promise and the prophecy of the Master, of all masters of all time. Acknowledge It; in all thy ways acknowledge Him—in *all* thy ways. When you get out of bed in the morning, acknowledge that you, of your own self, could not have done it. If you are awakened out of a sound sleep, acknowledge that you would have gone on sleeping but for an inner prompting that awakened you. And if you are awake and go to sleep, acknowledge that an inner urge, an inner prompting, gave you this rest. If you are successful, acknowledge that only the gift of God, the grace of God, could have made it possible. If you fail, acknowledge that only through a sense of separation from this *I* could there have been any failure, if failure it was. You may find that what appeared as failure was not failure at all, but only an experience to awaken you to your true destiny.

Acknowledge Him in all your ways, even when you have no evidence of the Presence. Agree that it is so even if you have not yet demonstrated it. As you persist in this practice and in your meditations, the day will come when you will feel a quickening within you. You will feel a peace that passeth understanding and you will know what spiritual rest means. You will know, in some way, that the Christ has come alive in you, that the Christ has been born or has been awakened in you. From then on, you woo the Christ. Hour by hour, woo the Christ; pursue It; acknowledge It; recognize It; step aside so that It can do a little more while you do a little less.

The day will come when this Presence will be such a living reality that most of the time you will be consciously aware of it. When you become too busy, It may recede into the background, but then a moment of not busy-ness will come, and It will again be with you. If the busy-ness is too intense and you seem to have lost It or to have become separated from It, you will find that deeper meditation will restore It to your conscious realization.

It is this Presence, entertained in secrecy and silence, that draws unto us our own and unites us with all life, in love, understanding, mutuality, and co-operation. We are united in one brotherhood by an invisible bond. That bond is the Christ of me and the Christ of you, making us of one household. Ultimately, this invisible bond of love will become the relationship of the whole world.

Acknowledge Christ in the midst of you, and then acknowledge Christ in the midst of all individual being—human, animal, vegetable, and mineral. This same Christ permeates the weather, the stones of the ground, the bottom of the sea, and the very air itself. Acknowledge that you are never outside of the realm of Its bosom, Its protection, Its love, and Its care, Its direction, Its wisdom, Its strength, and Its health.

Illimitable Scope of the Activity of the Christ

As you dwell upon the scope of the activity of the realized Christ, gradually, will come the conviction that this realization of the Christ can be applied to every circumstance and condition that touches your consciousness. If a depressing report of some disaster comes blasting over the radio, or if you read in your newspaper of sickness, infection, or contagion in your community, you can bring to that situation the activity of the realized Christ. As you witness the realized Christ in action, performing Its function, not merely in something as close to you as your body, but as far away from you as the other side of your community, you will understand that this activity of the realized Christ can permeate the entire universe, dispelling the causes of sin, sickness, and poverty, wiping out of human consciousness false desires, false appetites, and false ambitions.

If you have the opportunity of witnessing fear dispelled in yourself or in someone close to you, you should be encouraged to go deeper in meditation that you may witness the realized Christ dispelling fear in the consciousness of whole communities and nations. You have only to watch the miracle in yourself and in your family as fear disappears to know what it can do for the world. When there is no longer fear in world-consciousness, there will be no wars. Greed, lust, anger, and false ambition disappear with the disappearance of fear. Fear is the basis of practically every sin that man commits, individually or collectively—personally, nationally, or internationally. We fear a loss of somebody or something. We fear a loss of something we value; we fear a loss of our property or of our nation's property; we fear a collapse of our economic system; or we fear a restriction of our freedom.

The activity of the Christ realized dispels fear in your consciousness and in mine. The activity of the realized Christ will dispel fear in your home or your business; the activity of the realized Christ will dispel fear in your community, but there must be the realized Christ to do this; and in this age it is you, and you alone, who are responsible for the degree of Its realization. Wherever there is a realization of the Christ, there will be liberty, experienced and known.

This is the message of The Infinite Way. This is the mission of The Infinite Way. It begins by realizing the activity of the Christ in your consciousness and in mine, so that you and I may be healed of our physical, mental, moral, and financial discords. Then It takes over our family life. The activity of the realized Christ in your consciousness and in mine must be a leaven in your home and in your business, and from there It must go out into the entire community— into capital and labor relationships, into local government, into national affairs, into whatever place there is a problem in this world to be met.

When, through the realized activity of the Christ, we have witnessed the overcoming of the discords of life, we take the higher step of The Infinite Way and begin the ascent above human and physical harmonies. We rise above the pairs of opposites; not only above ill health, but above good health as well; above poverty, but also above wealth; above discordant conditions as well as harmonious conditions into that realm of consciousness where only *God is*. Only in inner silence and inner stillness can God impart to us that which *is*. When we are willing to be a perfect transparency to receive the instruction of God, then God speaks in our ear and shows us the spiritual reality, the Christ. If we can be touched by this activity of the Christ so that we are willing to "die daily" for each other that our spiritual nature may be reborn, is there any limit whatsoever to the scope of the activity of the Christ, the Presence in you?

Now is come salvation, and strength, and the kingdom of our God, and the power of his Christ.[10]

CABLE FROM LONDON

When a statement in the mind becomes a feeling in the heart, you can know that God is holding your hand. Reading and hearing about God's grace is learning the truth, but relinquishing the desire to ask God for anything is putting truth into practice. God is not a power that is going to do something: *God is the something.* You cannot use God or Truth, but God can use you.

Making Friends with a Friendly Universe

Every once in a while, a spiritual gem of literature appears on earth which, when we ponder and assimilate it, draws us into the very heart of God. Henry Thomas Hamblin, not only my dear friend, but the friend whose hand touches every Soul he meets with healing love, has just given us such a pearl, greater than price, *Making Friends with a Friendly Universe.* This is a treasure which will make your heart sing as you realize that here, in this book, a man is giving you his life's experience of the Soul. He is sharing with you that which has made him England's beloved mystic. England is but the home of his body: His Soul, his love, and his hand are wherever you are, and you unite with his life as his precious words enter your mind and heart.

In this booklet, Mr. Hamblin quotes one of our favorite Browning passages:

> Thy love
> Shall chant itself its own beatitudes
> After its own life-working. A child's kiss
> Set on thy sighing lips shall make thee glad;
> A poor man served by thee shall make thee rich;
> A sick man helped by thee shall make thee strong.
> Thou shalt be served thyself by every sense
> Of service which thou renderest.

THE ART OF MEDITATION
Recommended for Lenten Reading

You will be interested to know that *The Art of Meditation*[11] has received special recognition in Protestant religious circles. Edmund Fuller, literary editor of the *Episcopal Church News* and reviewer for *The Chicago Sunday Tribune Magazine of Books*, has included *The Art of Meditation* in a list of twenty-six books especially selected for Lenten reading, a list which he was requested to compile for the Religious Publishers' group and which was published in *The Saturday Review of Literature*, March 9. *The Cleveland News* of March 4 points out that more than nine hundred adult-level titles of religious books were published during the year, an astonishing output in this field. *The Chicago Sunday Tribune Magazine of Books*, March 17, says that "this indicates an increase in serious, meditative reading by Americans." From this impressive number of books, *The Art of Meditation* was selected as one of the twenty-six books recommended for Lenten reading. It is interesting to note that not all the books on Mr. Fuller's list were current publications. Included in these twenty-six titles, were several classics of religious devotion which have stood the test of time.

COMMENTS AND REVIEWS

A program to guide daily meditation to suit each individual's needs.

Retail Bookseller,
New York City, December, 1956.

Joel S. Goldsmith, a writer and lecturer who is well known in Los Angeles, has turned out a highly significant book dealing with spiritual wisdom as distinguished from mere intellectual knowledge.

Today many people are praying for the purpose of getting something. Goldsmith holds that meditation should be undertaken without ulterior motive.

"The purpose of meditation," says Goldsmith, "is to attain divine grace ... but we can never receive the grace of God so long as we seek it for the purpose of demonstration, that is, seeking God in order to possess some person or thing, or to achieve some place. That is the reason meditation can never be used to demonstrate an automobile, more money, or a better position; meditation is for the purpose of realizing God."

On the subject of meditation for healings, Goldsmith states, "As long as we are merely trying to exchange physical discord for physical harmony, we can have no conception of what the kingdom of God is, of spiritual riches, or of spiritual health. We must begin our meditation with the recognition that neither health nor wealth is the object of our search for God."

One more quotation which illustrates Goldsmith's approach to a significant subject is this, "Any meditation that has within itself a single trace of a desire to get something from God or to acquire something through God is no longer meditation."

Of Goldsmith's previous books, the best known is *The Infinite Way*. A previous resident of Hollywood, he has been lecturing in Europe, Africa, and Australia, as well as the United States, but spending much time in Hawaii.

Walter L. Scratch. "The Scratch Pad",
California Citizen News,
Hollywood, December 17, 1956.

This book may not be an immediate best seller. But in the long run it will be, for *The Art of Meditation* is destined to be a classic, a book which will endure along with other great spiritual works.

It treats of the necessity of meditation in learning the nature of God and in contacting God through prayer.

The author, Joel S. Goldsmith, says that the world, on the whole, does not know God; that if it did, its anguish, its wars, its sin and death would vanish.

True, he says, there have been men and women throughout the ages who have known God, have had conscious union with God; among these, Moses, Elijah, Jesus, John, Paul. But, on the whole, the author writes, we have no knowledge of God as the living Power and Presence with whom we are one.

But, he continues, individuals can learn the nature of God and how to contact Him so effectually in prayer that they will be helped into full redeemed life.

While such prayer is possible, the task of achieving it is difficult, according to the author. But he instructs the reader, in simply couched manner, how to realize truth. He writes in part: "Christ buried in the tomb of the mind will not come forth and do works, but Christ risen in our consciousness, Christ raised from the tomb through meditation and communion—that is the miracle worker of the ages."

Mr. Goldsmith says that the seeker for God must first learn His nature and that this may be done by contemplation. And, as patterns for our guidance, the author has presented many meditations which, he believes, if studied and taken into individual consciousness, will raise it to a high place. Then, in some quiet moment when all human thought is stilled, when all the noise and confusion of human living is hushed, in some moment of pure humility the God-experience comes in. And never again is that individual quite so grossly human.

Continued practice of meditation will result in the Christ taking over, Mr. Goldsmith writes. And when the Christ takes over, the individual, according to the author, is not, thereafter, subject to human ills.

The author is becoming widely known as a teacher of things spiritual. He lectures and has classes in the United States, England, Scotland, Holland, South Africa and Australia.

He is the author of previous books, among which are *The Infinite Way, Living the Infinite Way*, and *Practicing the Presence*.

Merab Eberle. *Dayton Journal Herald*,
December 13, 1956.

This writer gives contemporary expression to the mystical affirmation that God is indwelling, nearer than hands or feet, a very present help ... those who are ready to give heed will discover Goldsmith with joy ... [There is] thoroughness of conviction in the reality and power and sufficiency of God. Such conviction is an impressive thing, and for those able to share in it a most strengthening one. Goldsmith effectively sets aside distractions and insistently calls on one to be still and know the inexpressible.

Alfred C. Ames. *Chicago Sunday Tribune Magazine of Books*, January 6, 1957.

"Nobody," says the author, "could earnestly follow for any length of time the instruction in meditation as set forth in this book without noticing a change of a radical spiritual nature." When we have learned to value the Christ, we see Him as He is, "and God appears as the wholeness, the abundance, the harmony, the peace, and the joy of our experience." Author Goldsmith divides his exposition of meditation into three parts: The practice, the experience, and the fruits of meditation. He urges the reader to practice meditation at least twice daily and to turn to the kingdom of God within himself, to listen to the still small voice where "truth leaves the mind and enters the heart" becoming "a living thing within our being," the purpose being to attain divine Grace, to realize God, to turn from human things to the Infinite Invisible. With the object of listening to the still small voice one should consider any facet of spiritual truth proper subject for meditation. The most worthwhile part of the book is the section of ten meditations the author includes of "spiritual facets" he has chosen from Biblical texts. The fruits of our meditation will be spiritual living wherein we depend on divine guidance rather than human judgment. And, believes the author, those who recognize the Risen Christ should show others the way ... the book will be valuable to serious laymen for its way to meditation and the meditations in themselves.

V. Kirkus Bulletin. New York City,
February 1, 1957.

An able manual of introduction to the declining meditative art and an elaboration of its vital and productive role in Christian living and worship.

The Library Journal. New York City,
February 15, 1957.

✳ 6 ✳

JUNE

THE SECRET OF THE HEALING PRINCIPLE

SPIRITUAL HEALING IS based on an understanding of the spiritual principle of life. This principle is that God maintains and sustains the universe, including every person in it, in absolute integrity. Contrary to that teaching is the world of appearances, the dream world, a mesmeric world which has no law to support it, no substance to sustain it, and no continuity except such as we, in our ignorance, give it.

Once this truth is perceived, you will have a healing principle which will stand, regardless of the nature of the problems that are brought to you. This does not mean that you will heal everybody or every condition, not because the principle is not adequate to meet every situation, but because the people involved are not yet ready to *live* this principle or to live *by* this principle; they are not ready to give up those things which would interfere with the demonstration of the principle. In other words, Jesus, himself, did not attempt to take the rich man into heaven. It was not because of the man's wealth, in and of itself, but because the man's faith, confidence, and hope were in his wealth; all his expectations and hopes in life were based on the amount of his possessions, and such a man cannot be lifted into spiritual consciousness.

So it is that there are people seeking healing, but seeking only the healing of their pains and discords, not a spiritual healing which would transform their lives. This principle is so absolute, however, that given a fair opportunity with anybody who is at all receptive to the spiritual way of life, harmony will be brought into the experience of that person, and he will come into spiritual enlightenment.

The Fabric of "This World"

The principle which is the secret of all healing is an understanding of the nature of error. Error is never a person; it is never a thing; it is never a condition. Therefore, never take into your thought, or attempt to handle in thought, a person, thing, or condition. True, error always *appears as* a person or a condition, and that is what has confused the spiritual workers of the world. With every appearance of error, a rebellion, a resentment, or a battle against some person, place, circumstance, or condition is aroused in the individual, and the struggle is lost. No person on earth, or no group of people, is your enemy; no sin or no disease is your opponent or antagonist. The longer you fight a person, a disease, a sin, or a condition, the longer will you be embroiled in what we may call "this world."

You may believe that there is some individual or group of individuals standing between you and your harmony, and, to bring about a healing, you treat *them* or treat *for* them or treat that something be done *about* them. In other words, you are in antagonism, in resentment, in rebellion against them. Your efforts are directed toward them, toward removing them or bringing them into harmony, and in so doing, you lose your demonstration. It may not be a person, but some disease that is standing between you and harmony, and again you find yourself engaged in a battle with it and thereby dig your own grave.

People, things, or conditions are never the source of our discords. Let us be very clear on that all-important point. There is a universal force, a universal belief, a universal hypnotism which is the source of every discord that comes into our experience. Every limitation, every sin, every temptation, and every disease which come to us are but the effect of a universal force or power which, remember, in and of itself, is not power: It is only power because of the human mind's acceptance of it. If error were power, we could not dispel it. However, it is not power, except to world-sense. Universal belief is the only power which we have to consider in the meeting of sin, disease, death, lack or limitation, and it is not power.

To illustrate, let us take the case of a person who is dying. Now understand this: No person is ever dying. If you are ever called upon to help a person who seems to be near death, handle the age-old universal belief of a life apart from God, a life which has a beginning and, therefore, must have an ending. Do not try to save his life because you will not succeed; but handle the universal mesmerism of death, that universal hypnotism which says that everybody who is born must die. It is this same hypnotism which says that we were born, that we were created of matter, born of man and woman. The belief that you are a father or a mother or that you were born of a father and a mother is not a belief entertained only by you individually; it is not personal; it is a universal belief that has existed since time began. It is a universal belief in birth which results in a universal belief in death. What we are dealing with is not birth or death, but the universal belief, the universal hypnotism, which appears as an individual person who is dying, and this person could not appear to be dying were it not because of the original belief that that same person was born at some previous time.

Let us suppose that right now you are dreaming that you are swimming out toward the horizon. As you look around, you find that you have gone out too far and you are unable to make your way back. Now begins the struggle. You are seized with panic as you find yourself alone, struggling, far out in the water; but is there really a struggle? Is there water? Is there a "you"? What is the fabric and substance of the person you are seeing in the water? What is the fabric and substance of the water? What is the fabric and substance of the struggle? It is your dream, and only your dream. The dream is the substance; and you, the water, and the struggle are the objects which are formed by your dream.

If you were to take a piece of leather and from it fashion a man in one corner, a piano to the left, and a sky above, you would still have neither man, piano, nor sky: You would have leather. If you destroy the leather, you destroy the man, the piano, and the sky. With the destruction of the leather, the man, piano, and sky vanish. Just so, with the destruction of your dream, would the false belief of you in the water, the water, and the struggle, vanish. Now, in your dream of a life and death struggle in the water, if someone wakens you out of the dream, you would then discover that through the awakening or breaking up of the dream, automatically, would follow the breaking up of the "you" in the water, the water itself, and the struggle.

The fabric of the discords of human experience is a universal hypnotism, a universal belief. That is the fabric or substance of every sense of limitation that can come into your experience, whether it be limited finances, limited health, limited family, business, or social relationships, or any other discordant experience. The fabric of it is a universal hypnotism, a universal belief in a universe apart from God.

When Jesus said, "I have overcome the world," he did not mean that he had overcome all the people in the world and all the evils of the people in the world. His ministry was not of a long enough period of time to accomplish such a feat. But he did overcome the world, and in one stroke: by realizing that the only world that needed overcoming was composed of this mesmeric illusion. Then all the people, all the circumstances, and all the conditions of limitation disappeared.

A Universal Ignorance
Holds the World in Bondage

Let us remember that the ignorance that would separate people from a realization of truth is not personal to you or to me or to any of the people of the world: It is a universal ignorance, a universal sense of hypnotism which is always without presence or power. There is a universal ignorance which has gripped the mind of practically every individual on earth, making him unfriendly and antagonistic to truth. Why? Because truth received in consciousness wipes out the very things which humanhood has learned to love—the pomp and glory of personal selfhood, personal powers, personal strength, personal wisdom, personal glory, personal achievement. The human mind is in rebellion against anything which would destroy it. It resents hearing, "Why callest thou me good? There is but one good, the Father in heaven." The human mind is set on glorifying itself: "See my strength; see my wisdom; see my beauty; see my power; see my health; see my wealth: They are mine; I did that."

The universal ignorance which would separate people from understanding, apprehending, and demonstrating the message of The Infinite Way, is not a personal limitation; it has nothing to do with a person's education or his lack of it, with his religious training or his lack of it: It has to do with a universal ignorance, a universal mesmerism which is forever without presence and without power. Do you follow that? You are always dealing with a universal mesmerism or hypnotism which is the fabric of this world; you are not dealing with the pictures that the fabric presents but with the fabric, or hypnotism, itself. This realization is your saving grace. In other words, we never have a dying person to save or a diseased person to heal. We have a state of universal hypnotism, appearing as a sick, sinful, dying, or dead person. We never have an evil person; we have a state of universal hypnotism or ignorance appearing as an evil person. The moment we realize that, the evil person disappears, and we are able to behold him as he really is.

To become resentful of a person or a condition, or to battle a person or a condition is to become embroiled in it, to be ensnared by it. There is only one way to escape from this delusion of sense; there is only one way to escape from evil of any form in the world—evil people, evil thoughts, evil plans—and that is to stop battling it and to realize that behind it is the dream fabric of which it is constituted, and that that dream fabric is illusory, having no creative principle since God did not create it. Therefore, it has no existence or law to sustain it, no substance and no continuity. This realization destroys it. There is no clearer illustration of this than that of a dying person because it is extreme: We have no dying person to be saved; we have only an illusory sense of death. When we handle death from that standpoint, the dying person leaps up and says, "Here I am, all new, strong, and well." You have not done anything to a dying person, because the dying person did not exist to begin with; you have destroyed the fabric of the appearance, the fabric of that which was appearing. There is no other way of overcoming "this world."

This vision, this unfoldment, came to me while reading the life of Buddha. Gautama, who later became the Buddha, happened one day to see a sick man, a corpse, and a beggar. He was horrified that such things could exist. In life, as his father had arranged it for him, no such things were allowed to appear so that he had never witnessed any of these tragedies of human existence. He asked his counsellor, "Are these the only cases like this in the world?" When he was told that everyone eventually comes to this end, he was shocked; it was unthinkable that in such a beautiful universe as he had known, disease, death, and poverty should mar its harmony. That is the question that came into his mind and it gave him the clue to the whole problem: "I must find out how to remove sin, disease, and death from the world." That was it. He never thought about going out and healing people; he never thought of going out and reforming people or enriching people. His only thought was: How can I remove sin, disease, and death from the world?

The Infinite Way message is a revelation of how to remove sin, disease, and death from the world, how to remove the ignorance which separates people from truth. In The Infinite Way, people are only incidental to our ministry. The actual ministry itself is the removal of ignorance, sin, fear, death, and limitation from the world; and that is to be accomplished, not by going out and getting enough money to make everybody a millionaire, not by having enough wars in the world to kill off a sufficient number of people so that there are fewer to feed; but by breaking the entire mesmerism of limitation, ignorance, sin, fear, disease, and death.

You have heard me state that, when I am asked for help, I never take a person or his condition into my consciousness. This is the reason: The person or the condition is the decoy that would deceive the practitioner. To be a help to anyone, stop thinking of the person and the condition and realize that these represent only a picture, an image, or an appearance, the fabric of which is universal belief, this universal dream called the mortal dream, called the universal illusion, called by many names. It makes no difference what name you use for it as long as you realize that it is a universal sense which, in and of itself, has no law to sustain it, no cause, no effect, and no person through whom to operate.

"This World"

We are never going to solve our individual problems any more than we are going to solve national and international problems by trying to change people, heal them, reform them, or enrich them. We are only going to bring harmony to our individual world by seeing every discordant person, thing, or condition as a picture produced by this illusory substance called the dream of human existence, universal illusion, universal hypnotism, or universal belief, or, if you like, universal nothingness, appearing as people and conditions. Never try to save a dying person; never try to enrich a poor person; never try to cure a diseased person. Remember always that you are dealing, not with a person, not with a condition, not with a thing, but with a hypnotic suggestion, with a hypnotic influence, with a hypnotic picture, which has no existence outside the human mind, human belief, human appearance. In this realization, you destroy the entire fabric of which the error is made.

Every condition of limitation, whether it is limited finances, limited health, limited morals, or limited living conditions, is but the expression of a universal hypnotism, a universal illusion, a belief of a selfhood apart from God, a belief of a cause apart from God, a belief of a life apart from God, a belief of a substance apart from God, a belief of wisdom or knowledge apart from God. This whole series of beliefs constitutes a mesmeric influence making us see limited persons, places, things, and conditions. You can break up this Adam-dream into its component parts and you will find that the Adam-dream is made up of the belief of good and evil—the belief of a life apart from God, of a selfhood apart from God, of a law apart from God, of a substance, an activity, or a cause apart from God.

Every time you are called upon for the solution of a problem, notice that there is usually a person involved in it, but since God is the only creative principle, the child of God cannot be involved in any problem: The problem can only be the belief of a selfhood apart from God. Notice that every problem that comes to you comes to you as a condition. Can it be a condition of God? No, for if it were a condition of God, it would present no problem. The mere fact that it comes as a condition shows that it is an appearance which has no real existence, because actually there is neither a person nor a condition apart from God. Any appearance to the contrary must be a part of what is called the Adam-dream or the mortal dream or the illusory sense of existence, or what Jesus called "this world."

We should find it very simple to meet all the cases that come to us for help if we could merely say, "this world," and dismiss it with a smile, knowing that it is just a condition of "this world," the illusory world, not the real world, not

God's world. It is as if we were to go outside on the street and see children playing a game in which they had drawn a circle with their chalk on the walk, and then some child was imprisoned in it. The child in the circle cannot escape from his prison until something is done to rescue him. You, however, instead of attempting to extricate the child from his prison, look at him, smile, and say, "Ah yes, but that's the child's world," and walk on, knowing that in reality he is not imprisoned. If you can become accustomed to the idea that everything that appears in any limited sense, whether it is a person, or a condition, is a part of "this world," meaning the dream-world, the Adam-world, the unreal world, and then walk right on past it, you would soon discover how quickly the illusion is broken for your patient, your friend, or your relative.

We witness some untoward condition or some evil person, but if there is a God at all, there can be no such thing as an evil person, place, or thing. The difficulty is that we first see it and then we seek to do something about it, and in so doing we become embroiled in it. If, however, we see it—whether the "it" is a person, place, or condition—and then remember that the fabric of it is the dream, the illusory sense of a universe apart from God, or "this world," and then pass it by with, "Oh, that's just 'this world,'" we would break the dream. We break the dream of limitation the minute we ourselves become dehypnotized.

I have said to you that this is the year our students must be more diligent in breaking the mesmeric sense which binds them to human beliefs, and this can only be accomplished by learning the principle that there can be neither good nor evil in effect. Accepting good or evil perpetuates the dream. In your previous metaphysical studies, you have learned that all error is illusion, but in The Infinite Way you must go a step further and realize that the finite sense of *good* is just as illusory. You attain this consciousness through realizing daily that there is neither good nor evil in form, but that Spirit is the underlying reality of all. Try to understand that it is the belief of good and evil that perpetuates the dream and keeps you out of the Garden of Eden.

A practitioner is a person who, in some measure, is dehypnotized, who, to a degree, is not afraid of appearances and does not stop to fight them. Out in the world there is sin, disease, and death. Your non-practitioner looks out and says, "Oh, how terrible!" If, however, the practitioner has really arrived at a practitioner-state of consciousness, he looks out and says, "Tch, 'this world,' hypnotism, nothingness," and goes right on about the business of living.

There is only one thing impeding harmony in our personal experience, and that is this universal sense of a life or a selfhood apart from God, or of a law apart from God. There is only one way to break that sense of limitation, and that is to withdraw from the battle in the world, to withdraw from battling and opposing people and conditions.

Living the Christian Life

To live the Christian life means to accept the teaching of the Master: Love thy neighbor as thyself, but above all love the Lord thy God with all thy heart, with all thy mind, with all thy soul. These commandments are nothing but meaningless platitudes, until we begin to take them apart in our own minds and arrive at an understanding of them. How do we love the Lord our God with all our heart, with all our soul, with all our mind? What does it mean? Each one of us may have a different explanation and experience, but to me, to love the Lord thy God with all thy heart means not to love any form unduly and never to hate or fear that which is in the physical or mental realm—to place all faith in the Infinite Invisible as the reality of life appearing outwardly as effect. To come into a realization of the depth of the meaning of that statement requires a great deal of study. In not loving, hating, or fearing that which appears in the physical or mental realm, we break the mesmeric dream of a selfhood or a universe apart from God.

To love our neighbor as ourselves is to acknowledge that God is the Selfhood of all real being. God is the Selfhood of all individuals on the face of the globe, even when they are appearing as sick, sinful, or dying humanity. God is the Selfhood, God is the life, God is the intelligence, God is the law of all persons, even when in the mesmeric dream they may appear to be sick, sinning, or stupid humanity. To love our neighbor as ourselves means actually to acknowledge God as the very being of all that appears, regardless of the mesmeric appearance that is confronting us.

When we follow those two commandments literally, we can readily see that the entire appearance we are beholding of sick, sinning, stupid, dying, ignorant humanity is created by the world-dream, that which the Master called "this world." When this becomes clear to us, we shall never love these pictures, nor shall we hate or fear them. We shall not love the people in this world any more than we shall hate or fear them, but we shall love that which constitutes people: God, the Christhood, the Spirit and Soul of every individual on earth. That is the only way it really is possible to love "this world," because you will find it impossible to love the appearances that people present to you. If, however, you will look through these appearances to that which they really are, that which really constitutes their being, you cannot help loving everyone, whether he appears as man, woman, child, or whether it appears as animal or insect. Once you have perceived that there is an invisible Soul which is the real being of everyone, then you are able to look right through the appearance, to look right through the eyes to the very Soul which sits behind those eyes.

Resolve loving your neighbor into a spiritual activity. Behold love as the substance of all that is, no matter what the form may be. As we rise above our humanhood to a higher dimension of life in which we understand our neighbor to be pure spiritual being, God-governed, neither good nor bad, we are truly loving.[1]

In training yourself to look through the eyes of people and animals as you come in contact with them, you will automatically come to that place where you are no longer loving, hating, or fearing the appearance-world, or what Jesus described as "this world." In proportion as you can do that, you can say with certainty: "I have overcome this world. I no longer hate it or fear it or love it; I no longer try to get rid of it; I no longer try to fight it or battle it; I see through it— through it and behind it. I see that which really is: Godhood. I see that that which appears to be is but an image in thought made up of the fabric of a dream-world."

This is the secret of all secrets; this is the secret of spiritual living; this is the secret not found in the literature of the world. When you read most inspirational literature, although you may find it inspiring, you usually find yourself having the same problem to face tomorrow. The inspirational literature of the world, in and of itself, is not enough. It may lift us up and make us receptive to the Spirit, but it does not provide the truth necessary to our unfoldment. That truth is the truth that the discords, limitations, and inharmonies of this world are of the fabric of illusion—"this world," nothingness. In that recognition, you will have the secret of overcoming—overcoming "this world."

TRAVELOGUE

As you know, I had expected to spend the year 1957 at home in Hawaii, but the Father had other plans for me. *The Kailua Advanced Class* seemed to serve as a spur to forthcoming events, and soon arrangements were made for a trip to England and the Continent during April and May. Those of our students who study the tapes of *The Kailua Advanced Class* will understand that after attaining an understanding of this message, no one can ever again rest in material peace or human good. The message recorded on these tapes will become part of a book which is already in preparation for publication.

This brings to my thought the means by which spiritual teaching reaches human consciousness. From earliest times, those who have been instruments through which truth has come in new forms, have found themselves surrounded by serious students who have formed the inner circle and have become the active workers in carrying the message to human consciousness. A spiritual teacher receives the message, and he is able to impart it to the "twelve," the "seventy," the "two hundred"; but these can receive it only because of their devotion to the spiritual cause. In turn, these receptive students become centers around which other groups are formed. Always the spiritual message is prospered; its devoted students are important parts of a world-work, and become immortalized—though sometimes martyred—because of their spiritual zeal and their love of spiritual adventure.

We find such students with us all over the world: in Hawaii; in Canada; in San Francisco, Los Angeles, Portland, Seattle, Denver, Kansas City, Chicago, Detroit, Cleveland, Cincinnati, Louisville, Washington, D.C., and New York City. In the British Isles there are similar groups in London, Blackpool, and Manchester, England; in Edinburgh, Scotland. There are others in Holland, Sweden, South Africa, and Australia.

In Chicago and in New York this last March, I spoke to just such groups of our devoted and serious students, and observed that soon we shall probably require a theatre in each of these cities to accommodate the large groups who gathered to hear the message. In both of these cities, our students numbered from two to three hundred, a wonderful nucleus for the work—if, by their lives, they testify and bear witness to the power of this truth. You know that I have never sought enormous audiences or large numbers of people, but have been satisfied with just such small groups as you form. To you, I can impart the letter and the Spirit; and you, by your example, by the fruitage in your lives, and finally by healing, must carry The Infinite Way into the mind and heart of mankind.

Two years ago, I had a deep spiritual experience in Edinburgh, Scotland. During a visit to the castle, the buildings and grounds became illumined and transparent. It was a vision of reality—the world of form made of the substance of Spirit. Driving along the Royal Mile and up to the castle of Queen Elizabeth II, this transparency continued. It lasted almost until evening and lifted me above material discords and mental inharmonies.

Last week, on the same spot, at the castle in Edinburgh, another beautiful experience came which must be shared with you. The high priest of a spiritual order came to me and shared the joys of his order with me. He presented his priests and showed me their home, their estate, and their manner of living and working. He told me of their unbroken history dating back to the year 1078, and explained the goal of their work. In their life, is found none of the poverty or scrimping which is often associated with the usual concept of the monastic life. There is a bigness to their living, in home and estate, a bounty and an abundance, but not a wastefulness.

They generously shared their spiritual secret with me and showed me their way of practice and prayer which differs very little from our own work in healing. Their secret is our basic principle which—and perhaps not accidentally—is the subject of this June *Letter*. It was because of the similarity of our message and work that I was granted the unusual privilege of sharing their consciousness of truth.

The people of Scotland are, by nature, a religious people, and, potentially, a great mystical people. Centuries of lack— of limited resources—have gradually brought them, as it has most people, to the materialistic belief that their abundance and prosperity are dependent on trade and money. Such a belief often impoverishes those who cling to it; whereas, spiritual vision has always revealed that trade and money are abundant when dependence rests upon the Invisible rather than upon the humanly tangible. The work of this religious order, which is an unseen activity of prayer, has no doubt contributed to the peace and security of Scotland. The people themselves, however, in Scotland as everywhere, must open themselves to see their heritage of infinite abundance in Spirit before they will behold its tangible effects in the form of prosperous commercial and agricultural activities.

It is a state of mesmerism that binds people to the belief that their good is in the external realm of effect. Awaken to the truth that the kingdom of Allness is within you, never separate or apart from you, never to be struggled for—only to be realized. May your faith and trust always rest in the Infinite Invisible that your days on earth may be joyous, healthful, prosperous, and free.

❖ 7 ❖

JULY

SUPPLY

THERE IS ONE aspect of the subject of spiritual living and spiritual healing, which puzzles every beginner in the work. Not only does it confuse the beginner, but it perplexes many people who have made some strides upon the spiritual path; and yet it is a subject which never enters the thought of those who are well advanced in spiritual awareness. That subject is supply. It puzzles everyone in the beginning, because not only is it a difficult subject to understand, but it is also difficult to see how it is related to the spiritual life. Supply is something the beginner is often overly eager to demonstrate, or, through lack of understanding, refuses to think about because to him it is not spiritual, and, therefore, unworthy of consideration by a serious student on the spiritual path.

Of course, nothing could be further from the truth. As a matter of fact, there is no higher subject in the whole kingdom of heaven, nor one more closely related to the entire spiritual life than that of supply. Sometimes, as the student progresses in his study and work, he tends to push the subject of supply away from him because now it would appear that his mind ought to be on something higher, something more noble, something more spiritual. For the student who is far along on the spiritual path, supply is no longer a matter of concern, because with an understanding of the subject comes a knowledge of *what* it is. It has become so much a part of consciousness that it requires no conscious thought.

The beginner is confused about this subject because he believes that supply consists of money, property, investments, or business. These things are not supply: They are the products of supply; they are the visible evidence of supply—the out-picturing of supply. Supply is a spiritual subject, a deeply spiritual subject; it is the most spiritual subject you will ever encounter, because supply is the realization of God. It is an activity of truth which takes place within you and within me—a state of peace which descends upon us when the Spirit of God is felt within. It is this awareness of the presence of God which constitutes supply.

Supply externalizes itself as books, music, inventions, or new ideas of commerce; but these things in themselves are not supply: They are the evidence of supply. It is that deep peace, that stillness within, that becomes evident as supply in your experience. It would be well-nigh impossible for you to invent anything, to write an enduring piece of literature, or to compose a soul-stirring bit of music, if first you did not find a depth at the center of your own being—a deep pool of contentment within yourself, a deep realization of peace.

It makes no difference whether you call this realization God, whether you call it Spirit, whether you call it life, whether you call it a sense of peace, or whether you call it joy, as long as you understand that it is a feeling at the center of your being, a feeling which brings a smile to your face. Call it by any name you choose, but by whatever name, it is God; it is the Christ; it is the Spirit; it is Immanuel, or God with us.

Supply can never be found in the external world. All our young students who are trying to demonstrate supply in the external world fail because it cannot be found there. Supply

is within you; it is within me; it is within our consciousness. The very sense of peace and joy or the feeling of God's
presence that we may experience at any given minute is our
supply. Tomorrow, next week, next month, or next year, it
may appear outwardly as a new home, a new position, or a
new investment; but that will only be the externalization of
the supply which has been realized in a moment of peace.

There are still many people in the metaphysical world
who think of the demonstration of money, position, home,
or opportunity as something to be attained through struggle
and hard labor in the world. They act on the assumption that,
out here, there is money; or out here, there are homes; or
that, some place out here, there is opportunity; and that, by
praying or by engaging in some kind of mental hocus-pocus,
they are going to draw these things to them. That is the type
of metaphysics that leaves the student with a headache, with
mental strain, or with a sense of fruitlessness and frustration.
Even in those few cases where, in some mysterious way, such
mental effort results in the attainment of the desired goal,
there frequently comes the realization afterwards that this
was not what should have been desired or that it does not
meet the need for which it was sought.

In Isaiah we read: "Their land also is full of idols; they
worship the work of their own hands, that which their own
fingers have made."[1] Money is one of the idols made by men's
hands. Not only do men worship it, but they fear the lack of
it. In other words, they place their faith and confidence in
money and they give it power. But, actually, what power is
there in the work of man's hands? Is not all power in God?

Our individual consciousness is the storehouse of infinite
spiritual unfoldment. The moment we begin to draw from this
inexhaustible storehouse, which never takes account of what is
in the visible world, we cease being concerned with how much

or how little we have, or with whether the current economic status of the world be one of prosperity or depression. God has given to us infinite bounty, and it is unlimited in its expression, as long as we recognize that the earth is the Lord's, the silver is the Lord's, and the gold is the Lord's. It is only when we are trying to get our share of the world's goods, believing that the earth, the silver, and the gold are personal possessions, belonging to human beings, that we are limited.[2]

Money, in itself, is not evil, but a very practical and necessary commodity to be used as a means of exchange. It is as much of a necessity in our present-day civilization as are shoes, dresses, suits, or other items of clothing. But who worships, fears, or hates clothing? There are many things made by the hand of man that are desirable—houses, automobiles, airplanes, clothing, money, securities, property—all these are desirable but only as commodities to be used, not as something to be worshipped or feared.

The moment you begin to realize that the invisible Spirit is the health of your countenance, the moment you begin to realize that this invisible Spirit is not only the source of your supply, but is your supply itself, the moment you realize that this invisible Spirit, God, the Father, is your high tower, your fortress, your hiding place, your abiding place, your every need will be met.

Be sure of one thing only: Never regret the absence of any person or the lack of any thing. Never, never, never regret the loss or lack of anyone or anything in the outer realm. Abide in the secret place of the most High. Then you will never lack, because you will carry with you your supply of opportunity, your supply of ability, your supply of skill in art, literature, or whatever it is you wish to bring forth into expression. You carry your supply with you when you understand:

God is my deliverer; God is the essence of my being; God is. If I know nothing else, but that God is, that is enough, since my whole hope and faith are in the Invisible.

Those who have this vision become a light unto all the rest of the world, and of them the world may well ask: "Why is it that you are so favored? Why is it that you are so blessed with all the good things of life?" And their answer will be: "It is the free gift of God, but it is a gift that comes only to those who recognize God as the source, the essence, and the law—only to those who have turned from the visible realm to the Invisible."

Our Consciousness of God Is Our Supply

Ultimately, everyone on the spiritual path must understand the subject of supply through the spiritual vision which recognizes that there can be no supply in our outer experience unless there is a consciousness of God or good within our own being:

Right here and now, is the source of all the supply there is in the universe. Right here and now, is the substance, the activity, and the law of all the supply there is. Right here and now, the place whereon I stand is holy ground—whole, complete, and perfect. My individual consciousness is the source of all supply; it is the law of all supply; it is the activity of all supply.

Spirit is supply; life is supply. No one has ever seen life: Life is revealed through its forms, but life, itself, is never seen—only the forms bearing witness to life. The rose garden bears witness to life; orchards, filled with fruit, bear witness to life; animals bear witness to life; and we, ourselves, bear witness to life. But we have never seen life, itself, through the faculties of sight, hearing, taste, touch, or smell. Only those know life, only those have seen life face to face who can withdraw from the five physical senses, rest deep within their own being until they transcend the reasoning mind, and then with their inner eye and inner ear, with inner spiritual discernment, they witness life—almost, it may be said, they see God while yet in the flesh. There is a Soul-faculty, a spiritual discernment, which enables us to know the things of God and to know that they do exist; and then, knowing that, to realize them as the tangible forms of our everyday supply.

The entire message of The Infinite Way is based on the principle that the Word becomes flesh, the invisible Spirit becomes manifest, realized or made evident in our daily experience as the form of bodily health, mental health, and economic security, not by a seeking of these on the outer plane, but rather through the realization of their true nature.

The realization of the true nature of supply does not mean that we should stop working, but that we stop working *for a living*. We work, but we work for the joy of the activity; we work for the joy of beholding perfection. "Man, whose breath is in his nostrils,"[3] has to sweat to earn his living, but not spiritual man. His living does not come through toilsome labor. The spiritual man works hard—he may work as many as twenty hours a day and work hard during those twenty hours but he does not work for a living; he works for the satisfaction and joy he finds in the work itself. The spiritual man knows that the invisible Spirit is the source of his living, that his heavenly Father knoweth that he has need of these things even before he does, and that it is His good pleasure to give him the kingdom.

The man grounded in Spirit may be a very prosperous and a very healthy person, although the possession of either property or health is no indication of spirituality; but such a man does not put his hope, his trust, or his confidence in storehouses full of gold, because these are effects, neither good nor evil, in and of themselves. His confidence is in the Invisible, that which the world cannot see. The world cannot see the Invisible, and that is why the world is in trouble. "But ye, my disciples"—you catch the spiritual vision, you know that there is an Invisible, and your hope is in It, your confidence is in It.

Resting in that spiritual vision, you can undertake whatever your work is with joy and freedom. You are not free *from* anything; you are free in the realization that the work of your hands is love. You do your work with love and you do it to the utmost of your capacity, not for the sake of competing with anyone, not for the sake of winning any glory or honor, but for the sake of the work itself.

Abundance Is the Law of the Universe

There is an invisible Spirit which is forever appearing as form on the visible plane. In the autumn, the fruit on the trees is plucked, and the leaves drop away, but nobody is alarmed. Everyone knows that nature is at work, and that in a few months the leaves and the fruit will reappear. This we all know, but we fail to recognize the analogy between this cyclic activity of nature and our own supply. Sometimes when we look into our pocket-books and find them empty, the mesmerism of the world is so great that we think we have come to the end of our supply. We forget that just as there appears to be a season of barrenness in the life of a tree, so we, too, may pass through a period of lack which is only a temporary phase in our total experience. Within us, deep within, that same law of God which, through Moses, brought manna, a cloud by day, and a pillar of fire by night, that same law which brought ravens with food to Elijah, which multiplied loaves and fishes, which has always fed, maintained, and sustained those of spiritual vision, that same Spirit is here and now in the midst of us.

That Spirit which so abundantly fills the earth with its fruitage, the sea with fish, the air with birds, the hills with cattle, the ground with every sort of vegetable, fruit, and flower, in such abundance that it cannot be counted, provides all good for us. Abundance is the divine plan for us, but we have missed it in looking at the outer forms and trying to lay them up "where moth and rust doth corrupt,"[4] feeling that, if we do not hold them securely in our grasp, there will never be any more, instead of enjoying that which is set before us, in the realization that the Infinite Invisible which we call Father, Spirit, or God, has provided for us an infinity of supply when we look to It.

Many people have experienced lack for such a long period of time that they actually believe that there is a law of limitation binding them to the experience of lack. This belief that there is a law of lack is the first suggestion which must be broken. If you could count the birds in the air and the fish in the sea, or if you could swim down under the Pacific Ocean, as we do out here in Hawaii, and could count the shells, the rocks, and the flowers that grow underneath the water, you would know that there is no such thing as a law of lack. Abundance is the law of the universe.

Abundance is supported by law, and therefore, abundance is a permanent dispensation. It is something that is as eternal as it is infinite. Count the stars in the sky and the drops of water in the ocean; count the leaves on the trees; and then understand what infinity really means and you will know what abundance is: It is the law of life—infinite, eternal. There is no law of lack and limitation.

Supply Becomes Tangible as Form

How, then, are we to realize the tangibility of that supply which we already recognize to be infinite? Begin by relaxing all effort; drop all sense of strain in considering the subject of supply. Whether the need is for the supply of some truth or the supply of the tangible forms of this truth as it will later appear, learn to relax. Relax, not only physically, but mentally, in the realization that you can do nothing about supply. Jesus said, "I can of mine own self do nothing,"[5] and you surely can expect to do no more than the Master, who added, "The Father that dwelleth in me, he doeth the works."[6] What is this Father within, except the infinite, divine, universal Consciousness, which is your consciousness and mine? That is the Father, that is the principle, the creative principle of all forms of supply.

Form the habit of reserving a space within your consciousness to which you retire every day for two, three, four, or five minutes, and there realize:

God, all these things which I behold are but the outer forms of my supply, but Thou, and Thou alone, art my supply Thou art my protection; Thou art my high tower; Thou art my fortress; Thou art my bread, my wine, my water; Thou art my daily manna. The forms as which my supply appears are unimportant; the essence is in Thee—in God, Spirit, Love.

Supply is not an external thing; supply is an invisible substance which you can never see with your eyes. If you were writing this monthly *Letter* and wanted to finish this particular article, you would have to become aware of supply. Something would have to flow forth as a supply of words. But where will you find the words, except as they flow out of consciousness? That is true of the supply of all things. It rises up from out of the depth of your own consciousness and flows out into tangible expression. As you stop thinking of supply in its outward form and begin to think of supply as an inner, invisible substance, as something already established within your own being, you can rest from mental labor and even from a large measure of physical labor. That does not mean that you will stop working, but your work will not be labored; it will be joyous and pleasant, whether it is physical or mental work.

Behind the mental or physical work, will be a conscious pouring through of the Spirit as of a feeling of peace, contentment, assurance, and satisfaction enveloping you. As you live in that consciousness and let that consciousness live in you, truth begins to flow out into form just as these words are taking tangible form. Remember that before these words were written down, they were an invisible form in my consciousness which later appear in visible form as lectures, *Letters*, or articles. Before anything can appear in visible form, it has to be in the consciousness of an individual in its invisible form.

There is an invisible consciousness of Truth within me, built up over the centuries, and that invisible Truth is now externalizing itself in these words as this particular message. That is the form that my consciousness of God takes—this message, these words. It was in exactly the same way that Thomas Edison embodied within his consciousness knowledge which made him an electrical and mechanical wizard. When he reached back into his consciousness, a practice which he indicated by his typical gesture of holding his hand up to his ear as if he were listening for an inaudible sound or trying to receive a message, Edison was reaching far back into his consciousness for supply. In his case, it was for a supply of ideas, for a supply of wisdom, for a supply of knowledge.

This consciousness of Thomas A. Edison then externalized as a phonograph, a motion picture, or an electric light.

So it is with our great musicians and authors. They sit listening, listening, listening—for what? For that invisible something, that inaudible something, hidden deep within them. Then, in a flash, the inspiration may come, and they quickly seize a brush, a pen, or a piano; and the visible evidence of the supply that was in them appears as a painting, a book, or a symphony.

The same thing is true about your business, your home, your relationships, your investments, your safety, or your security. These, you will find, first, by adopting this listening ear as if there were something deep, deep down inside that had to come through. It is that inner supply that reaches you on the inner plane which later becomes visible as your daily supply, your daily occupation, vocation or avocation.

Supply Becomes Tangible as Healing

This same supply becomes evident as healing. No spiritual healer can heal anyone on the external plane because he never touches a patient's body; he never uses any form of manipulation; he never prescribes medicine or external applications; never does he approach, even in thought, his patient's body. And yet miracles of healing take place. How? In this same way. There is a depth within that we know as God-consciousness or Christ-consciousness or spiritual consciousness. When the human mind is still, when we are not trying to think thoughts or get favors from a Santa Claus-God, but when we are really and truly still and at peace, It wells up from within, and the result of It is a feeling as of a weight dropping away. When that happens, the practitioner smiles, and the work is done.

The patient, a mile away or three thousand miles away, experiences that same feeling of release, even though he does not know the practitioner is working for him at that minute. At one particular moment in the work, it may be in the first treatment or it may be in the one hundred and first treatment, but at that moment when the practitioner has a deep enough feeling of God's presence within, the patient, being attuned, responds to it, feels that divine impulse within him, and the healing takes place. There, again, supply has been demonstrated. First, it had to be a supply of God-consciousness. Then, it appeared outwardly as a supply of health and painlessness; it could even appear as a new body where that is necessary.

At whatever stage you may find yourself in this spiritual journey, you must take that word "supply" and hold it in front of your eyes until you gain an understanding of its real significance. Do not be afraid of it; do not think you are dealing with some lowly, material thing, because there is no material supply. All supply is spiritual. Only do not think in terms of the forms of supply such as money, property, homes, or investments. Think in terms of the essence of supply: Spirit is supply; your God-consciousness is your supply; the activity of Truth within you is your supply. Remember, too, that it is just as important for the healthy person and the wealthy person to recognize the invisible nature of supply as it is for the sick person or the poor person. Wealthy people, if their sense of wealth is in material values, are no wealthier than the dollar bills they possess or the ground they own, both of which are subject to fluctuation and change. There is no security in the wealth of the wealthiest or the health of the healthiest, except as they carry with them this recognition: "Thank you, Father, for this outer evidence of an invisible supply." Then their supply, whether it is of health or wealth, is grounded on the rock and it will never desert them. The man of vision is not relying on an external condition but is attuned to an invisible substance which is forever flowing from the within to the without.

You can never measure the extent of your supply by the external evidence. There is only one way in which you can judge the amount of your supply, and that is by the amount of God-contact you have achieved within you. That contact is the infinity of your supply. You can draw on it for plots to write books, music to write compositions, or new designs for buildings or bridges. Anything that you need for some outer activity, you have by virtue of the fact that you have achieved a realization of the supply of the substance of it within you. Once you have the substance within you, that is, the realization or the feeling of the presence of that substance, everything you need on the outer plane is provided. These are the added things.

Supply is an inner state of being; it is an inner quality like integrity. You have never seen integrity, but you have seen the results of integrity in your conduct in the outer world; you have seen the outward expression of that invisible essence that appears as deeds of honesty, loyalty, fidelity, justice, mercy, or kindness. In the same way, if there were no inner supply, there would be no externalization in the form of dollars or property or income. If there were no inner essence or substance, there would be no outer expression or form.

If this is true, why is it that there is lack and limitation in the world? If supply is omnipresent and exists in the consciousness of every person, why is there anyone on earth in lack? The omnipresence of supply is the consciousness of God within, but it becomes visible, evident and tangible, first of all, in proportion as we know the truth that Spirit is supply, Love is supply, and that these are not visible, but that they are the divine Presence and Power within us which externalizes Itself as the forms of supply.

Realize the Christ-Peace

There is a peace, "*My* peace," which becomes our supply of health, wealth, harmony, joy, and dominion. Until we arrive at that "*My* peace," the Christ-peace, the abundance of life eternal cannot appear in manifestation. It is true that life is eternal; it is true that supply is infinite; it is true that safety and security and joy are here and now; but you and I cannot experience them until we have touched that "*My* peace" which *I* give, that inner, spiritual peace.

There is only one way to have the peace that passeth understanding; there is only one way to have an infinity of supply, perfection, and health, to have a complete assurance of safety and security; there is only one way, and that way is that Christ dwell in your heart:

I am in Thee and Thou art in me; we are one. The Christ lives and moves and has Its being within me; I live, move, and have my being in Christ; and we are one in God.

As we know this truth intellectually and sit in patient receptivity, an awareness that passes knowledge steals over us. It is above knowledge: It is a feeling, an intuition, an inner assurance, a release, a divine peace. When that comes, we are filled with the fulness of God, and it is literally true that the kingdom of God is within us. It is then that the fulness of the Godhead bodily is established within us. In that awareness, we know that God will never leave us, never forsake us, never abandon us. Even in our sins, the Father will still be with us, awaiting our recognition and awakening.

The reason all people are not experiencing health, wealth, harmony, safety, and security is that they have not consciously turned within to receive this divine grace or peace. They have the peace which the world can give, but they have not turned within: "Father, I await Thy pleasure. 'Speak, Lord; for thy servant heareth.' "[7] They have not sat in silent, inner communion, until they received the assurance of divine grace and heard in their ear:

My peace I give unto you ...[8] I will never leave thee, nor forsake thee.[9] Whither thou goest, I will go. ...[10] I will be a Presence going before you, making the crooked places straight.

Sit in quiet, at peace—not going to sleep, not in blind faith, but alert, awake, receptive—until the contact is made. It is in that quietness that the Holy Ghost overshadows you; there is a stirring within you, and you know, "This is It." This is the peace that passes knowledge; this is the peace that is above any truth there is to know.

Acknowledge "I Have"

Begin with the understanding that you have.[11] Acknowledge that you have, whether it is a few loaves and fishes or some oil in your cruse; acknowledge that you have some understanding of God; acknowledge that you have some measure of love for God and man; acknowledge that within you is the kingdom of God; acknowledge that the place whereon you stand is holy ground. The evidence on the outer plane may be that you have not. But in your acknowledgment that you have, you are ready for the continuous flowing from that cruse of oil or the multiplication of the loaves and fishes. Now you can let that cruse of oil continue to flow or the loaves and fishes continue to multiply themselves, until everybody is satisfied and there are twelve baskets full left over. But this can only come about if you realize:

I have. Thank you, Father, I have. All that the Father hath is mine. I seek nothing on the outer plane; I desire nothing on the outer plane; I pray for nothing on the outer plane. I acknowledge that all that the Father hath is mine, and this allness is within me. The kingdom of God is established within me; the place whereon I stand is holy ground. I already have the kingdom of heaven within me; I and the Father are already one. I am not praying to be at-one with God; I am not desiring to be at-one with the Infinite or in tune with the Infinite. I acknowledge that the relationship between Father and Son is an eternal one: "Son, thou art ever with me"[12]*—not sometimes, but always.*

Hold fast to this truth in your consciousness and even though you walk the streets tomorrow without a bit of food or a place to lay your head, still hold to this truth:

I have *some oil in my cruse. I* have *some loaves and fishes. Even though I cannot see them, I have them because I am one with God. The Father will never leave me nor forsake me: As* I *was with Abraham, Isaac, Jacob, Jesus, John, and Paul, so* I *am with you. I* was *with you from the time before Abraham was, and* I *will be with you until the end of the world.*

Hold to "I have," and to that "I have" will be added. That is the spiritual law about supply; that is the secret of supply. God is your consciousness; God is your Soul; and therefore, it is your consciousness which is full of God, full of good, full of every kind of good there is. Be like Jesus: Just look up to the Father, or down to the Father—wherever you feel the Father may be, since He is both up and down, inside and outside—close your eyes, and rest in confidence: "Thank you, Father, the whole kingdom is within me."

JOEL GOLDSMITH'S NEW BOOK[13]

Henry Thomas Hamblin

I have been assured by the publishers that Joel Goldsmith's new book, *The Art of Meditation*, will be available during the month of June.

This latest book by Joel is undoubtedly the best book on the subject of meditation that I have ever come across. Very few people know what meditation is, and still fewer have ever practised it. It is an art that is far from being easy to master. Joel, himself, had a great struggle, but he persevered until at last he conquered all its difficulties, and that, doubtless, is the secret of his power and the basis of his inspiration. In chapter 5 he writes:

> Meditation is a difficult art to master. Were it not so difficult, the whole world would long ago have mastered its technique. In my own experience, eight months of from five to ten meditations a day were necessary, before I received the very first 'click' or sense of the Presence within—eight months of meditating day and night. Furthermore, I had no knowledge that such a thing as making a contact with God was possible, or that it would accomplish anything once it was achieved. There was, however, deep within me, an unwavering conviction that it was possible to touch something greater than myself, to merge with a higher power. Nobody whom I knew had gone that way before me; nobody had prepared the ground for me. There was only that inner conviction that if I could touch God, at the center of my being, It would take hold of my life, my work, my practice, and my patients. By the end of eight months, I was able to achieve one second of realization—perhaps it was not even one second. I do not know how to measure time when it involves less than a second, but it certainly was less than a second of realization. It was another week before the next second of realization came, and many days before the third one. A whole week intervened before the fourth moment of realization was achieved; then, it happened twice in one day. Finally, the day came when the realization seemed to last for an eternity and that eternity was certainly far less than a minute. It was probably three years before I

learned that if I got up at four o'clock, sometime between then and eight in the morning, I would feel that 'click' or awareness that God is on the field. Some days the 'click' came within five minutes and some days it took the whole four hours, but never after that did I leave for my office until the Presence had been realized.

Now there are never less than nine or ten hours out of the twenty-four given over to meditation—not in one single period, but five minutes at a time, ten minutes, twenty minutes, thirty minutes. There is no regular schedule.

The author then utters a word of warning, which all would do well to heed. He says:

As we advance in this work, if we permit ourselves to be deprived of our periods of contemplation, by the pressure of business or the demands of increasing responsibility, we shall miss the way. Once the Christ-center has been touched, it is possible that activities may increase to such an extent that they encroach upon the time which should be devoted to meditation. Too great an indulgence in the things of this world might soon take from us the spiritual gift which is infinitely more valuable than any material thing we may sacrifice. The Master withdrew from the multitudes to commune alone in the wilderness and on the mountain-top. We, too, must withdraw from our families, our friends, and our human obligations for those periods of communion necessary to our inner development and unfoldment. An hour or two of meditation or communion, with no purpose or desire of any kind, brings the experience of God to us in an ever-deepening measure.

At this point may I emphasize what Joel says about meditating without purpose or desire. This is most important. Some systems of meditation have an object in view, such as healing of physical ills. The meditation is practised solely in order to find healing, or release from some other human trouble. But true meditation (and I am glad that Joel teaches this) is directed to God alone and not to any human benefit which might be derived from so doing. Directly thoughts of physical or material benefit seek to enter the mind they should be dismissed, and the attention again directed to God. If this is persisted in, then as Joel so truly says, "the experience of God comes to us in increasing measure."

I want to emphasize another point, viz., that this book of Joel Goldsmith's is far from being "just another book on meditation"; indeed, in my opinion, it is unique and quite unlike anything which has preceded it. It makes previous works appear old-fashioned and out of date by comparison. Its teaching is profound and is the fruit of a wide experience. It is not theoretical, but, is exceedingly practical. Joel knows what he is talking about because he has come through deep waters; he, like your editor, has had to climb out of the deep pit with slippery sides and at last has got his feet planted on firm ground. His teaching is not for those who wish for an easier life here, but is for those who are determined to find God and enter into Divine union, at all costs.

This work is nicely arranged in three parts. One is devoted to Meditation: The Practice; Part Two, to Meditation: The Experience; Part Three, to Meditation: The Fruits. The next to the last chapter is entitled "Illumination, Communion, and Union." It is exceedingly wise and helpful. From it I quote:

> There is no limit to the depth of Christhood. Illumination leads to communion in which there is a reciprocal exchange, something flowing out from God into our consciousness and back again from our consciousness into the consciousness of God. It is meditation carried to a deeper degree than has been experienced thus far, but *we* do not carry it—God carries it. It cannot be brought about by any effort on our part; it cannot be forced. We can only be patient and wait for It and then find that It takes over and there is a peaceful, joyous interchange in which we feel the love of God touching us and our love for God returning to God.

As I have stated elsewhere, meditation (if mastered) leads to contemplation, and contemplation leads to Union and Oneness. We become changed into the likeness of That which we contemplate. As St. Paul said: "He that is joined to the Lord becomes one Spirit."

TRAVELOGUE

Travelling the entire world as I have been doing, it is impossible not to be aware of the great evolution which is taking place in consciousness. Through the development of electronics, machinery, and other mechanical and scientific advances, men are attaining an ever-increasing freedom from heavy labor and unending hours of work. Through the great progress made in labor-saving devices and household gadgets, women have been given heretofore unknown hours of freedom for more interesting and more creative activities. The lightening of the workload is evident throughout the world. Even in the industrially undeveloped countries, side by side with primitive farming methods, old-fashioned buildings and housekeeping, is the oncoming and incoming of the new age.

Man is also rapidly attaining freedom from the diseases of the world. In many places, tuberculosis hospitals are no longer filled to capacity; polio has been considerably reduced; typhoid fever, pneumonia, and a dozen other diseases have all but disappeared. Venereal disease, once the scourge of the earth, is being controlled and will rapidly disappear as new methods of treatment are better understood and applied.

With the growth of trade unions and the advent of social security, economic security has become more certain. The evils at present existing in these forms of human betterment will also be eradicated through the evolutionary process.

Man's material welfare is being well established in ways of peace and harmony. The evils of warfare are destroying warfare itself—and thus a permanent cessation of war is practically assured in the not too distant future. All these changes are apparent to every observant traveler.

In the area of man's spiritual development and his spiritual freedom, we find less progress. The Old Testament reveals how people developed spiritually under teachers of varying degrees of wisdom. Throughout the centuries, among these lesser lights, we occasionally find an Abraham, a Moses, an Isaiah, a Lao Tse, a Buddha, a Jesus, a Paul, and a John. Later came the European and Asian mystics bringing forth some measure of spiritual light.

Today man's evolution seems to lie primarily in the realm of the physical sciences—mechanical, chemical, and biological—while his spiritual development remains more or less stagnant under differing and competing forms of creed, doctrine, and worship. Travel the world over and you will notice how small are the groups surrounding the true mystics of this age. Notice, too, the difficulty there is in locating even those few. Man's spiritual development, bringing with it a freedom from material good as well as from material evil, is slowly penetrating human consciousness—slowly, *but surely.*

We who are bringing the art of meditation to light again, we who are introducing man to his inner Self, we who are charged in this age with restoring moments of inner peace, through meditation, and the accompanying power of grace—we have a great responsibility to our fellow-men, to our age, and to all future ages.

Man's eternal freedom from fear, sin, and lack—man's eternal health, harmony, abundance, and peace—can be assured *only* by contact with the Infinite Invisible within, a contact which must be attained and, thereafter, continually sustained. Upon us who have benefited by meditation and by the healing grace which comes with inner spiritual living—upon us, rests a responsibility and a privilege. If you have not yet realized the importance of your place in this world, in this age, and in the ages to come, *wake up*. You are important to the spiritual welfare of the universe. Be willing to accept this privilege; be willing to shoulder the responsibilities which it carries; be grateful that your names are writ in heaven and that you have been called upon to show forth your spiritual light.

Our work in England, Scotland, and Holland has been completed for this year. Glorious work it has been with dedicated groups which meet regularly to meditate, to study recordings of the class-work, and to bless all those who turn to them and also the many who indirectly benefit by their nearness. These groups around the world who share the sacredness of our class work are my hope for the enduring place of The Infinite Way in human consciousness.

In England, more titles have been added to the list of British publications. In Holland, *The Infinite Way Wisdoms* will appear in September as a separate book, giving us two books in the Dutch language. *I Am the Vine* has been published as a pamphlet in Norwegian. Thus is the message being made available to an increasing number of people. The work grows rapidly in South Africa and Australia through healings and uplifted lives.

Remember that some students *believe* that they are seeking God or Truth, when they are seeking only remedies. This explains many failures on the spiritual path.

✤ 8 ✤

AUGUST

Your Names are Written in Heaven

GOD IS ONE—one power, one presence, one law, one cause—and yet most religions acknowledge two powers, the power of good and the power of evil. Sometimes they are called God and the devil, sometimes mortal and immortal, sometimes good and evil. Always there are the pairs of opposites—truth overcoming error, Spirit destroying matter.

In the message of The Infinite Way, oneness is a principle by which anyone who undertakes healing work must rigidly abide. Since God is one, never under any circumstances is there a person to heal, a disease to cure, a sinner to reform, or a lack to be overcome. Only the person who holds steadfastly to the truth of oneness can bring about what we call healing, which really is not healing at all, but revealing: It is a recognition of Christhood as our true identity. We never try to get rid of an illusion; we stand fast in oneness. Since Christhood is our true identity, that recognition is the treatment, except for the final point of realization, without which no treatment is complete. We recognize the fact that in the human picture there appear forms of error, forms of destructive things and thoughts; but our work is the discernment of Christhood, of true identity, of one power, one being, one Selfhood.

In the earlier stages of our experience, this is a difficult practice. Well do I remember the very first month after it was revealed to me that *I* is God—the *I* at the center of my being, the divinity within me. This revelation came to me at a time when I was going through a very severe problem of financial lack. The revelation that the *I* is God brought with it a recognition that that *I* is Self-maintaining and Self-sustaining:

I is the source of all supply. I is not someone who gets supply; I is the very source and multiplier of supply. Therefore, I embody supply; I include it. Supply is embraced within my own being. Supply does not come to me; it flows out from me.

However, it was not more than an hour after that revelation came to me that someone asked me to pay a bill which I owed, and shortly thereafter, another demand came, and the next day another. Each time, I had to ask my creditors to be patient with me. Outwardly, I gave lip service to the appearance of lack, but inwardly, the recognition persisted that *I* is the source of abundance, *I* has sufficiency, *I* has abundance, *I* does not receive anything, *I* can feed five thousand.

The heavens did not open at once and pour down thousand-dollar bills, but steadily, bit by bit, standing fast in the recognition of this truth, harmony was restored. After truth has been recognized, it must be realized. That does not always come in an instant. It may take a year before one truth is thoroughly established in your consciousness, but you must persist in its practice until it becomes rooted and grounded in you as realized truth. It has been my experience that one statement of truth has occupied my consciousness for as long as two years.

Oneness is a supreme principle in this work, and it must be realized to the exclusion of all else until it is indelibly impressed upon consciousness. As long as we are trying to correct erroneous conditions, we are admitting that erroneous conditions exist. On the one hand, we acknowledge that there is a God and, on the other hand, we believe that God's universe has slipped out of God's control, and that it is our responsibility to patch it up.

There Is Neither
Good nor Evil in Form

All power is in God. That is the principle, but how can that principle be applied to the human scene when an individual is faced with a diseased body or a sinful person? The answer is very clear: There is neither good nor evil in any creature. There is no power for good or evil in any person, circumstance, or condition. At this particular moment, some of us are meeting with evil people, some of us with poor people, some of us with sinful people, and some of us with sick people; but that is only because we are accepting the universal belief in God and devil or in good and evil. All power is in God. If all power is in God, and God is invisible, there is no power in anything that you can see, hear, taste, touch, or smell. If you can see it, hear it, taste it, touch it, or smell it, it has no power; and what is more, the motivating power of that which we see, hear, taste, touch, or smell is an invisible substance called Spirit.

Let us return to our old familiar illustration of the hand. A hand is not good and it is not bad; it is just a hand. A hand cannot give and a hand cannot withhold; therefore, there is no generous hand and there is no stingy hand. A hand cannot love and a hand cannot harm; therefore, there is no loving hand and there is no destructive hand. A hand is a hand. If anything is to be done by a hand, the "I" to whom that hand belongs must do it. As a human being, I have the power to give or withhold through this hand, to love or to harm. However, when I surrender my humanhood and recognize that the *I* of me is God, this hand can neither give nor withhold:

I and the Father are one. The Father alone governs me, maintains me, sustains me, supports me, and animates me. God alone is my being. This hand can do nothing of itself: God alone moves it. I am not mortal man whose breath is in his nostrils; I am not a man conceived in sin and brought forth in iniquity: I am the Christ of God, the Son of the living God. Even my body is the temple of the living God. I surrender my body, my mind, my heart, and my Soul to God.

The realization that our body can manifest neither good nor evil, that even we cannot manifest good or evil, is what constitutes a true spiritual treatment. Let us not claim to be good, but on the other hand, let us not claim to be evil: Let us claim God as our identity; let us claim God to be the mind of us, the Soul of us, the Spirit, the law, and the cause. When we begin to understand that there is neither good nor evil in the creature, that is, neither good nor evil in anything that is created, anything that has *form*, anything that exists as *effect*, we have begun our rebirth. This rebirth, the dying daily of the old man and the rebirth of the new, can only take place when we stop trying to change forms. Let us stop trying to change the creature and begin to recognize that all form, all effect, is a visible manifestation of an invisible, creative Principle called God. All form is subject to the creative Principle that formed it, that sustains and maintains it unto eternity.

The hand loses its power to be good or bad and now becomes subject to God alone. So it is with every organ of the body. Can a heart be sick? Can a heart be well? No, a heart can only be a heart; it has no qualities of its own. A lung can only be a lung; a liver can only be a liver. Neither a heart, lung, nor a liver can be sick or well, good or bad, alive or dead. They have no qualities of their own. Whatever a heart, liver, or lung is or has, comes from the invisible Source which is God. The heart cannot keep anyone alive: Only life can do that, and life animates the heart.

Life governs the body. This will not be true in our experience, however, if we believe that we can have a good body. We shall only prove that life governs the body when we recognize that the body is neither good nor evil. The body can be neither sick nor well.

Give up the belief in good or evil; stop accepting the pairs of opposites. An example of the importance of knowing neither good nor evil is found in dealing with the problem of alcoholism. Too many people attempt to meet such a problem by declaring that alcohol is not evil; but that is not the belief from which an alcoholic is suffering. He is suffering from the belief that alcohol is good. You must recognize that alcohol is not evil because there is no power in anything which does not emanate from the spiritual Source, but that is not enough; you must also recognize that alcohol is not a power for good. That is the belief from which the victim is suffering: He is finding good in it, not evil. There is only one way to destroy alcoholism and that is in the same way in which the appearance of ill health is destroyed: There is neither good nor evil in form, in effect, in anything you can see, hear, taste, touch, or smell. That which has been maintained by the belief in good and evil disappears when we know that, whatever it is, it derives its qualities from an invisible Source, and that Source is God.

Disease continues because of the belief in good and evil. We believe that a body with disease is bad and that a body without disease is good. We try to get rid of the bad in order to have the good. It cannot be done. *There is no good or evil in form, in effect, in the creature.* "I will not fear: what can man do unto me?"[1] Why not? Because there is no power in mortal man or in his body.

Renounce the Pairs of Opposites

Another way in which we find ourselves ensnared with the belief of good or evil is in looking at people. We are always eager to unsee the evil man and delighted to see the good man; but all power, all life, is in God, and therefore, there is no good or evil in man. Stop trying to exchange bad people for good people. See through the disguise of both good and evil and behold Christhood. Do not fear the evil and do not love the good; look through both to Christhood.

Do not rejoice because your patient has been made well. We are not interested in a sick man or in a well man; we are interested in Christhood. Do not be like the disciples who ran back to the Master rejoicing that even the devils were subject unto them: Rejoice that your names are writ in heaven. Do not believe that truth overcomes error: Rejoice that it has been revealed to you that Christ is your identity, that you are the Son of God, heir of God, joint-heir to all the heavenly riches. Rejoice that your nature is spiritual and then you will not find any evil to be overcome. Never rejoice because a headache has been healed, or a cancer: Rejoice that God has been revealed as omnipresent. When God is revealed as omnipresent, it makes no difference what the appearance is, because no human belief can stand in the presence of God realized. Do not rejoice because the lame man leaps: Rejoice because God has been revealed as the identity of what appeared as a lame man.

The secret of spiritual living is the revelation that your names are writ in heaven, that you are spiritual—children of God: You are not good and you are not evil; you are not sick and you are not well. Look through the appearance to the Christ. Go beyond the pairs of opposites; do not try to overcome one with another. Know ye not that your body is the temple of God? Know ye not that you are heir of God and joint-heir with Christ in God? It is just that simple and it is this very simplicity which often fools us. We do not take these simple truths into our consciousness and drive them home until we actually come to the conviction of them.

There is no use in continuing to battle error. Realize your spiritual nature; stop fighting good and evil; stop trying to give up the evil to get the good. Dwell in the secret place of the most High with the great truth that God constitutes individual being and God is neither good nor evil. God is an infinity of Spirit, life eternal, immortality made evident. "Fear ye not, stand still, and see the salvation of the Lord... "[2] God is; God is one; God is good. If God is one and God is good, you have nothing to contend with: The battle is not yours. You will never succeed by might or by power; you will succeed only by grace. By grace are you saved. By the grace of God are you saved, but that grace comes when you give up your efforts to change evil into good. Give up every human effort: Give up your effort to use truth; give up your effort to think good thoughts instead of bad thoughts; give up all your efforts to believe that by taking thought you can accomplish anything. Give all this up and acknowledge:

My name is written in heaven. I can rest in the bosom of the Father. At any moment of the day or night, I rest in the Father's love. I hug to myself the realization: "All is well. My name is written in heaven."

I may take to my bed at any minute that it seems to be necessary and just hold fast to this realization. I may have to stay in that bed three days before I come to this realization; but if necessary, I shall do that, too. Or I may go off to a stream somewhere, to a mountain, or to the seaside, away from people, away from newspapers, and hug this truth to myself, not with a battle, but by just gently reminding myself: "My name is written in heaven. 'God's in His Heaven, all's well with the world.' "

There is nothing to be overcome; there is nothing to be destroyed; there is nothing to be rebuilt. The secret is that your name is written in heaven. If this temple that you call your body is destroyed, it will be rebuilt again in three days, a perfect, harmonious, whole and complete structure, functioning as God intended it to function. This you will achieve, not by power, but by the grace of God, by surrendering the belief that you have physical powers or mental or spiritual powers. Acknowledge that God alone is power. Only God is; and whatever God is, is what you are. Anything else is a dream-world based on a temporary belief in a selfhood apart from God. It is a universal belief—not yours, but only a belief universally accepted.

The experience of the prodigal is the effect of that universal belief. Did you ever stop to think that actually he never was a prodigal, that he was always the son of the king? Even when he was eating husks with the swine, he was heir to all the wealth of his father. So with you, regardless of the husks which you eat—spiritually, morally, mentally, or financially—you can never change your true identity. Your names are written in heaven. That is your relationship to God and that is your relationship to each other. Stop trying to become spiritual; stop trying to be holy; stop trying to gain wealth;

stop trying to get health. Your names are written in heaven. That is the principle of the Christ.

You have no power over evil. Give up the belief that there is evil and you will not meet it anymore, but also give up the belief in the power of good. Renounce the pairs of opposites because as long as there is a tiny bit of universal belief in your consciousness, it will manifest in some form. This point is clearly stated in the Wisdoms:

> Why do advanced Souls (even practitioners and teachers) still experience ills and other problems? Whatever degree of mortal or material consciousness that still remains in them is expressing itself. *There is no unexpressed consciousness*, and even a tiny bit of remaining human consciousness will express itself in terms of human good or evil. This is the law. These two remain side by side until, *in proportion* as spiritual consciousness unfolds, more and more of material sense is uprooted. Even the Resurrection brought forth a material sense of body, with all the marks of human error. In the Ascension, pure spirituality is revealed.[3]

The consciousness which is free of the belief of two powers is a light to those in darkness. Only those free of the belief in good and evil can perform spiritual healing.

"My kingdom is not of this world." When universal hypnotism is broken by the activity of the Presence, "this world" is no longer present as a problem, but merely as an accompaniment to life itself. Like background music, it is pleasantly there, but not importantly.

The Secret of Healing is Reaction[4]

The whole secret of healing lies in one word—reaction. There is nothing more loving than the Christ-ministry, and yet this Christ-ministry is completely indifferent to appearances, whether they be good or evil. Healing work requires not only intense love for God, but a great reverence for a God who can maintain such a perfect, harmonious universe. This love and reverence, however, must be accompanied by a total indifference toward every appearance that does not testify to the perfection and harmony of God's universe.

Your reaction, when a claim is presented to you, will determine the healing. If you can be indifferent to the appearance, you can be the instrument for a quick healing and a beautiful healing, depending upon the receptivity of the patient or student. If, however, you react with the tiniest trace of doubt or fear, thereby accepting the appearance, you may have a long battle. Our concern must never be with the appearance, but always with the principle. When asked for help, we do not dwell upon the physical condition of the patient and whether it is going to improve in an hour from now or six days from now; but our responsibility is to stand on the principle that God is the Soul of all being; God is the only law, the only power, the only substance, and the only activity.

We do not concern ourselves with the identity of the patient, or with the name or nature of the claim. We stand on the principle: Christ is the true identity of individual being. Christ is my identity; Christ is your identity. When we know that about a patient, it is impossible for us to have any anxious concern for him. Our function is a realization of God's government in individual life.

Almost all the sins and diseases of the world are the result of universal beliefs. For example, a person sits in a draft and catches cold. Why? There is a universal belief that sitting in a draft will give a person a cold. Another person becomes infected with some contagious disease because of a universal belief in infection and contagion. None of this has anything to do with the patient. Therefore, when confronted with any of these beliefs which have gained worldwide acceptance, remember that it is not a person and it has nothing to do with a person. It is a universal belief and is not a power: All power is in God.

Your function, as a practitioner, is to be still in Christ and let Christ's will be done on earth as it is in heaven. Whether you are handling problems involving business, capital and labor, or marital problems, be sure that you never enter the case humanly; never permit yourself to give human advice. Do not react to the appearance and never try to change the appearance. Non-reaction to appearances is a demonstration of your faith in God's ability to govern His own universe. Ignoring the appearance and centring attention on the principle is a matter of training and self-discipline.

It is not necessary to know the name of a patient or what is troubling him because these things do not enter the treatment at all. Our concern is the word of God which reveals that God is the principle of this universe; God is the principle of all creation; God is the life and the mind and the Soul of all being:

I and the Father are one, and all that the Father hath is mine. All of the divine consciousness of the Father is the divine consciousness of me, because we are one. All of the spiritual power of God is the spiritual power of me. I am an instrument through which this power is pouring forth to the world.

As you work with this principle, gradually you pass from an intellectual perception of the principle to the consciousness of it. Never again is it necessary to make a declaration of truth, but truth is continuously pouring through you. "I, if I be lifted up from the earth, will draw all men unto me." And what does it mean to be lifted up? If I am lifted up to that place in consciousness where I have no concern about any person or condition, but where I understand that God really is the Soul of the universe and the governing influence—the only influence—then I am abiding in the principle. It is a recognition of the truth that God is the central theme of existence; God is the life; God is the all in all.

Even after we have become thoroughly grounded in the principle, temptations are going to come to us for quite some time. We shall be tempted to believe in a selfhood apart from God, to believe that we do not live and move and have our being in God, to accept a sense of separation from God, to accept sin, disease, death, lack, and limitation as actual states of being that must be overcome. When these temptations come, the remedy is at hand:

Thank you, Father; I am home in Thee. I am now in the secret place of the most High. Right now, in spite of this appearance of being in the valley of the shadow of death, right now, I will fear no evil, for I and the Father are one. All that the Father hath is mine.

The greater use you make of the word *is* or of the word *am*, the nearer you come to the realization of true being. "The Lord is my shepherd; I shall not want." We do not have to make the Lord our shepherd nor yet search for a shepherd, but just realize: The Lord *is, is, is* my shepherd; I shall not want. Face any appearance of a lack of safety or security with that truth. When we abide in Truth and let the word of Truth abide in us, that is our remedy for every temptation.

Since we already live and move and have our being in God, we do not have to seek or search for remedies, for treatments, or for prayers. All we have to do is to sit still, or stand still, or lie still, and realize: "Thank you, Father, it is done." Be not afraid. In any situation, "be not afraid; it is *I. I* am in the midst of you; *I* am with you; *I* will never leave you nor forsake you."

Remember, only as we consciously accept this in consciousness, do we make it tangible in our experience. As long as we entertain a sense of separation, as long as we acknowledge that we are somewhere outside of God trying to get back into God, as long as we are seeking to bring God into our experience, we are continuing that sense of separation. Instead of accepting a sense of separation, "lean not unto thine own understanding," but acknowledge Him in all thy ways and he will give thee rest:

Though I make my bed in hell, Thou art there with me. God in the midst of me is mighty. I am; I already am; and that which I am seeking, I already am. I am in the secret place of the most High. I am about my Father's business.

My eyes are closed to discords and inharmonies, to appearances and temptations. I do not see and I do not hear evil. Even though I see the appearance of evil, I do not accept it as reality. I see it as a shadow, which I neither hate, love, nor fear. I behold God alone, God appearing as the life of all being.

Never give power to appearances; never react to appearances of either good or evil; have no other gods, no other power but the One. From The Infinite Way standpoint, there is not truth over error, or God overcoming evil, but the realization that there is no power in any evil appearance for God to overcome. There is no power in form; there is no power in any effect or condition: All power is in the Infinite Invisible. That is the healing principle.

Comments on *The Art of Meditation*

Starting with the conviction that man is not alone in the world, Joel S. Goldsmith is concerned with man's need of prayer. Prayer—the art of meditation—has to be developed and he introduces the reader to a daily program of meditation which will help him to realize his oneness with God and to find a clearer view of himself and his world.

His book is divided into three parts, Meditation: The Practice; Meditation: The Experience; Meditation: The Fruits. It will help the reader to achieve freedom from bondage to materialism, from addiction to small and unworthy ends, and from all forms of self-seeking. Careful instructions, illustrative examples and specially written meditations are all fully set out for the reader seeking spiritual guidance.

Joel Goldsmith is a spiritual leader who is becoming increasingly known in many parts of the world. He lectures and conducts study groups in the United States, England, Scotland, Holland, Sweden, South Africa, and Australia. Recognized as a teacher and healer, his message is becoming increasingly known through his writings. He has also written *The Infinite Way, Living The Infinite Way, and Practicing the Presence.*

George Allen & Unwin Ltd.,
London, England.

An able manual of introduction of the declining meditative art and an elaboration of its vital and productive role in Christian living and worship.

The Christian Century,
Chicago, Illinois, March 13, 1957.

A layman who has developed his own technique for religious meditation and inward prayer outlines the practice, the experience and the fruits of this spiritual discipline. It rests on the conviction that man is not alone in the universe and that a mystical awareness of God is something that can be cultivated by a persistent daily program.

Religious Book Club.

This new Infinite Way book reached me as a gift from Mr. Goldsmith at Christmas time, and I am most grateful, for it was so timely, inspiring and helpful.

In introducing this book to our readers, I suggest that they think of it not so much as just another book, but as a textbook which challenges them to practise the art of meditation.

Those of us who know Mr. Goldsmith, will recognize that here he is sharing with us the inmost secret of his own soul's experience. So many books have been written about meditation. It has been the theme of the mystics in all ages; but here in this book, meditation is not discussed as a theory, but as a possible joyous and rewarding experience. It begins with these words, "Most men and women are convinced that there is a divine Power of some sort operating in human affairs; but they are not sure what it is, nor do they know how to bring this divine Presence and Power into daily experience." *The Art of Meditation* is written in explanation of how this "inner Presence" can be realized and used in daily life.

The writer refers to the mystics of the world explaining that they each became rays of light, flowing to the world in need, from the central source of all wisdom. Christ located the kingdom or consciousness of God within the human life when He said, "The kingdom of God is within you." He spoke of this inner witness as "the Father within" saying, "I of myself can do nothing, the Father within me doeth the works."

The secret of the art of meditation is revealed in the art of listening, which is accomplished only by relaxing the outer reasoning, thinking, planning mind (this is the only mind which most of us know anything at all about). It is when this outer mental process is still, that we can begin to understand what is meant by "the art of meditation."

The author makes it clear that the student will be tested in his search, and explains that attainment comes only by and through perseverance and patience, and the refraining from the use of mental effort, and cultivating the stillness and entering the calm of the spirit.

The purpose of this helpful, simple book is to release to man his God-given birthright, which includes freedom from bondage to materialism, and from bondage to small and unworthy ends and self-seeking. The book is divided into three parts.

Meditation: The Practice

Meditation: The Experience.

Meditation: The Fruits

I can only introduce the book to the readers of *The Seeker* in this short article. I do suggest that you each obtain a copy and keep it by your bedside for quiet study.

A. S. Webb. The Seeker,
Perth, Australia, March, 1957.

ACROSS THE DESK

Do you remember that toward the end of 1956, or the beginning of 1957, I told you that 1957 would be the year of fulfilment for the message of The Infinite Way? Now I can say to you that the prophecy, if such it was, has come true: This is the year of fulfilment for the message of The Infinite Way.

Jesus gave the world this Messianic message: There is a transcendental Presence and Power within the consciousness of every individual on earth, and this spiritual Presence and Power he called "the Father within"—your Father and my Father. He taught and proved that this spiritual Presence and Power heals the sick, unstops the ears of the deaf, opens the eyes of the blind, feeds the hungry, raises the dead, and gives spiritual illumination, so that the enlightened live not only by bread, but by an inner meat, an inner wine, an inner water, an inner bread of life which Jesus revealed as the grace of God. In other words, the grace of God, the activity of God's presence and power in us, is our daily bread, our supply, our activity, our wisdom, and our immortality. Throughout his three-year ministry, he proved every single point of this teaching by healing the sick, bringing forgiveness to the sinner, demonstrating supply, and revealing immortality.

The disciples and apostles, and later their students, were able to prove the omnipresence of the Spirit of God in man and Its redemptive power; they broke the mesmeric Adam-dream and revealed that "henceforth know we no man after the flesh." In other words, no longer shall we believe in a good human being or a bad human being, but in the under-standing of this spiritual Presence, we shall know all men as the Sons of God or offspring of God, the spiritual heirs of God—the Christ. This teaching was lost when men began to observe ceremonies and rites, arguing and disagreeing about the form of worship and eventually dividing into numerous sects, each with its own form of worship, ceremony, and creed. Attention was focused on the form rather than on the Spirit, and the essence was lost.

In this past century, it was again revealed to the world that there is a Power always present and available in individ-ual consciousness; and spiritual healing and redeemed lives were the effects—the proof that man shall not live by bread alone but by every word of Truth that is entertained in con-sciousness. Throughout the world, there have been followers of Christian Science, of Unity, of Divine Science, and more recently of The Infinite Way, who have taken the word of God into their daily experience and have placed their hope, their faith, and their reliance on the Infinite Invisible and have proved that the spiritual life is the most practical way, the most productive of harmony in human affairs.

With the advantage of all that has been learned in the metaphysical field during the past three-quarters of a century, together with my many years of experience in the healing work, The Infinite Way now is presenting to the world the correct letter of truth on which man can build a foundation for spiritual awareness. The Infinite Way is a restatement of the spiritual truth that there is a Father within, that which Paul called the Christ, through which and by which man can live. It reveals the principles of spiritual healing, principles which each one must know if he hopes to bring the activity of spiritual healing into his own experience and into the experience of others.

Until recently, however, only those on the metaphysical and spiritual path of life have been able to benefit by these revelations. Since The Infinite Way has been presented, it has proved itself so completely, not only as a spiritual teaching, but as the correct letter of truth on which the actual demonstration of spiritual living and spiritual healing can be based, that our work has gained recognition in the Protestant churches of the United States and Canada. In fact, the entire Protestant world has opened itself to the acceptance of the revelation of spiritual living and spiritual healing, based on this teaching. This means that within a few years there will no longer be just a few metaphysical organizations practicing spiritual healing, but that this teaching of the Master will now become a universal activity.

Students, I have lived for this day—the day when I would see the churches accept the spiritual way of life. Now a greater duty becomes yours, for now you will have to take part, or rather you will have to take a greater part, in bringing this message to the world. Therefore, this month, develop the healing work using the June, July, and August *Letters* as your guide. In these three letters, you have the basis from which to give your treatments. Practice the healing work.

❖ 9 ❖

THE PRAYER OF MYSTICISM

LIKE MANY WORDS, the term "prayer" has no absolute meaning, in and of itself. Prayer means one thing to the child who says, "Now I lay me down to sleep"; it means another thing to the person who unthinkingly recites the Lord's Prayer in a monotonous drone, "Our Father who art in heaven hallowed be thy name"; and it means something entirely different to the person who reverently prays, "Our Father—which art in heaven—Hallowed—be thy name."[1] That is as different a sense of prayer as is the Twenty-third Psalm, "The Lord *is* my shepherd,"[2] a prayer which is an acknowledgment of that which God is, that which God does, and that which God means in individual life. Still another prayer is the prayer of gratitude, the "thank you, Father," which is a recognition that all good is in, of, from, and through the Father.

Let no one have a static sense of prayer. Let no one in The Infinite Way ever say, "This is prayer, but that is not prayer." That which we may feel is a very deep prayer today may seem very far from prayer a year from now. On the other hand, a year from now we might know something entirely different about prayer from what we know today. There is no such thing as a right form of prayer or a wrong form. Every prayer that has ever been voiced is right from the standpoint of the consciousness voicing it at the time. The form of prayer used by a person one day may be entirely different from the form used by the same person on another day. This does not mean that all prayer is effective, but if our prayer is sincere, it represents our sense of right at any given moment—the best we know at that moment.

The highest form of prayer that has been revealed in the religious literature of the world is that in which there are no words and no thoughts, a form of prayer which is entirely a listening attitude, a listening as if to receive the word of God, which is quick and sharp and powerful. God is; perfection, omnipresence, omnipotence—all this already is; and therefore, there is no need to pray to God for anything.

In the allness and isness of God, what does prayer become? How do we pray without praying amiss? Those of us who are engaged in the healing work must realize by now that there is no treatment, and there never has been a prayer or a treatment that we or anyone else can give that would heal anything or anybody. There are certain forms of prayer or treatment which we might use today to elevate ourselves to a state of listening consciousness so that we become receptive to the word of God, but it is the word of God which heals, reforms, improves, and supplies: It is not any treatment that we give; it is not any prayer that we voice. This does not mean that we will not give treatments or that we will not pray, nor does it mean that we will not think. It means that we will recognize when we are treating, praying, or thinking, that the purpose of treatment and prayer is not to influence God; it is not to persuade God to do something.

The moment we go to God with any idea of expecting God to do something for us, we are trying to influence God to move out of Its orbit. We are not satisfied with the way that God is functioning; and therefore, through prayer or treatment, we are trying to change that which God is or that which God is doing. There is no better way than that for us to lose our entire demonstration.

Certain it is that human beings may be influenced to act differently; certain it is that they may be an influence on each other to improve their mode of living or their concept of what is right to do; but surely, no one could believe that *God* can be influenced. God is already the infinite intelligence of the universe: Let us not try to tell that infinite Intelligence what to do or when to do it. Let us not try to tell God what our need is, or our neighbor's need, or our family's need because, if we succeeded, we should only prove that God is not omniscience, that God is not the all-knowing wisdom of the universe. Jesus taught that we are not to take thought about what we shall eat, or what we shall drink, or wherewithal we shall be clothed, nor are we to turn to God for these things. Our heavenly Father knoweth what things we have need of.

If we follow the Master's teaching closely, we shall find that in no place did he tell God what he needed; at no time did he pray to God to send him what he needed. His prayer was the realization that the Father in heaven knew that he had need of these things and that it was His good pleasure to give him the kingdom. He taught us how we could be abundantly supplied with food, clothing, and housing when he said:

> Take no thought for your life, what ye shall eat; neither for the body, what ye shall put on. ...
>
> For all these things do the nations of the world seek after: and your Father knoweth that ye have need of these things.
>
> But rather seek ye the kingdom of God; and all these things shall be added unto you.
>
> Fear not, little flock; for it is your Father's good pleasure to give you the kingdom.[3]

We have nothing to do with prayers for things; we have only to do with seeking the kingdom of God, the realization of God. That is our whole function in the spiritual life—never to ask God for anything, never to try to tell the all-knowing God something that we believe God does not know, and more especially not to ask a God of love for that which it is His good pleasure to give us. When we pray to God for things, we are virtually saying, "Now, God, I know more than you do about my life, and not only that, but I want you to be more loving than you are because at this moment you are withholding those things that I am sure I need; and so now I am trying to urge you to be a little more loving and more thoughtful and considerate of me and send to earth these things that I am sure I need, but that you do not know that I need—or if you do, you are sitting up there withholding them."

Only One Demonstration Is Necessary

Every time we pray for something, it is an indication of our lack of faith in God and our failure to understand the true nature of God: We are denying God's infinite wisdom and His everlasting love; we are denying the nature of God as infinite intelligence. God constitutes the world; God embraces the world; God includes the world within Itself; and when we have God, we have the world. We cannot have God *and* a lack. Therefore, there is only one demonstration for us to make and that demonstration is the realized Christ. Then, whether our need be mental, moral, physical, or financial, whatever is necessary will be added unto us; actually, it will be disclosed as part of our very being, but it will appear outwardly as if it were being added unto us, as if it were coming from somewhere external to us.

The more we try to demonstrate supply, the less we shall have of it; and the more we attempt to demonstrate health, the less of it we shall have. There is no supply and there is no health, in and of themselves, because both health and supply are qualities and activities of God. The only way to get health or to get supply is to get God, and then we shall find that health and supply are included in God. Therefore, let us let loose—let loose right now—of all attempts to get health and supply, companionship, home, or opportunity; let us stop trying to demonstrate anything or anybody. Let us center our whole attention on seeking the realization of God. Our prayer or our treatment must begin with the premise that God already knows what things we have need of, and it is His good pleasure to give us the kingdom.

As we abide in the conscious realization that it is the Father's good pleasure to give us the kingdom, we shall not try to influence God. We shall open our consciousness so that the infinity, the wisdom, and the love of God may find an outlet through us. As long as we think of prayer or treatment as a means of elevating ourselves to that state of consciousness in which we can be receptive to the activity of God, or an instrument for the activity of God, then the prayer or the treatment can take any form that suits us at the moment; but the very moment that prayer and treatment are used for the purpose of enlightening or influencing God, then prayer and treatment are amiss.

We do not go to God for anything,. since we are no longer seeking the opposite of what we seem to lack. We are neither seeking to rid ourselves of evil, nor are we seeking to gain good. Now we have only one purpose: to seek the grace of God—the realization of God's presence and power. If we understand this, our life will never again be the same, our desires in life will never be the same. We shall be able to bury that old creature, that person with desires, that person with wants, that person with lacks and limitations. We shall bury that person and be reborn of the Spirit.

The old creature which is always in need of health, supply, or companionship will never die while we are feeding its desires. This old creature is not the man born of Christ; he is not the man born in the image and likeness of God. The new creature born in Christ needs nothing, prays for nothing, and rests always and only in the bosom of the Father, rests in the realization of spiritual integrity and spiritual being. This new creature is not man who needs redeeming, but the Son of the most High, at home in God.

Can you imagine spiritual man praying for anything? Can you imagine spiritual being needing anything? Can you imagine spiritual being seeking anywhere outside itself? Spiritual being knows that "I and my Father are one,"[4] that "the place whereon I stand is holy ground,"[5] and that "all things that the Father hath are mine"[6] because "I am in the Father, and the Father in me."[7] Spiritual being knows the completeness of its spiritual nature and seeks nothing, but rests—just rests—in the shadow of the Almighty, under His wings. That is all spiritual being ever does—just rests:

I am in the Father, and the Father is in me. I and the Father are one; all that the Father hath is mine. Thank you, Father, for Thy being, Thy presence, Thy grace. Thy grace is my sufficiency in all things.

What kind of prayer are we using? Are we praying from the standpoint of a mortal who wants to become immortal, of a mortal who wants better mortality, *or* from the standpoint of a realization of our true identity? Each form of prayer represents our state of consciousness at a given moment. When we believe that we are mortals seeking immortality, we must find some satisfactory form of prayer that will help us achieve our end. If we are mortals with not enough health and insufficient wealth, then we shall continue to pray for a little more health and a little more wealth and be satisfied that we still be mortals for three-score years and ten.

Die Daily to Humanhood

When, however, we begin to glimpse a ray of spiritual light, one of the first things we learn is that we are made in the image and likeness of God; and as that image and likeness, we are one with God, heirs of God, joint-heirs with Christ to all the heavenly riches. Then our entire sense of prayer changes, and prayer becomes a continuous realization of God's presence until the day arrives when we are not so much interested in material good—material health or material wealth, fame or fortune: All we want now is the realization of spiritual grace. "My grace is sufficient for thee."[8] When that time comes, we no longer pray for health, knowing that health itself may be of short duration; but, with no desire for human good, we let our mortal selfhood die—die daily. Most of us are willing to die daily to our sins and diseases, but how about dying to our health and our wealth; how about dying to all these things and resting in spiritual grace, spiritual fame, spiritual fortune, spiritual integrity, spiritual wisdom? How about actually following the Christian teaching of dying to our humanhood and being reborn of the Spirit?

I do not know how high we can go in spiritual demonstration. The Wayshower set the example of complete Christhood. That is the goal. The achievement may be something less than that, but we shall not even achieve "the something less than that" unless we know what the goal is and strive to reach it. We are not making a real attempt to attain the stature of manhood in Christ Jesus as long as we are praying for material good, whether it be material health or wealth. The measure of the stature of manhood in Christ Jesus is not a good man and it is not a healthy man: It is the Son of God, eternal in the bosom of the Father. A healthy man is not even closely related to spiritual man. A wealthy man is not even on the fringe: Sometimes, as the Master indicated, the wealthy man may have no possibility whatsoever of attaining heaven. If we place material wealth before us as our goal, we ourselves are putting up the barrier to our own entrance into heaven; whereas, by dying daily to the desire for human betterment, and by praying, meditating, and communing with God for but one purpose—the realization of His grace and presence—we shall not only be supplied with all good on the human plane, but one day we shall begin to understand what the nature of spiritual man is.

It is a far cry from this present moment to the old metaphysical days when we *used* God to attain some form of material good. It is a far cry from those days when we prayed to God for just a little more health, just a little more recognition, a little more peace—peace of mind, peace of body, peace of Soul. To be a follower of the Christian teaching of dying daily to our humanhood is not easy, but no one who has put his foot on this path can turn back: Once he has put his hand to the plough, there is no looking back. There may be pain, struggle, and stress in taking the next step; there may be a great many hardships in going up one more rung of this ladder, but the hardships will be only temporary because once we have taken those first few steps, we begin to get wings.

From this point on, we become as indifferent to health as we are to sickness: We can no longer work *for* health any more than we can work *against* sickness; we cannot work for supply any more than we can work against lack. At this stage we lose our interest in the pairs of opposites, and we behold Christhood. We may fall down many times in applying this principle, but it is a glorious principle. It is a glorious principle which enables us to turn away from health and supply, and say with absolute conviction, "These do not interest me. Christ alone is my vision. I do not work for health and I do not work against sickness; I do not work for supply and I do not work against lack: I realize that Christ, the one Selfhood, is my being—infinite, eternal, harmonious, and omnipresent." Then watch how the dead arise, how the sick pick up their beds and walk, how the lame, the blind, the deaf, the dumb, and the poor have the gospel preached to them.

God's Grace Is Our Sufficiency

The password at this stage of our experience is: "My grace is sufficient for thee."[9] It would appear, in some cases, that we need more health; but no, the password is, "Thy grace is my sufficiency," not health, but Thy grace. It might appear that the need is supply or greater abundance, but that is not true: Thy grace is my sufficiency. It may appear elsewhere that the human sense of sin has to be overcome and that greater purity is needed, but there, too, only one thing is needful—*Thy grace.*

In order to turn away from the attempt to demonstrate health, supply, companionship, or any of the things of human existence, we must keep that password locked up in us, but always available; so that when a problem of health for ourselves or for another, or a problem of supply, companionship, or home, presents itself, we can turn from it and not try to demonstrate its opposite. Let us drop the pairs of opposites and demonstrate that "My grace is sufficient for thee."

We, in The Infinite Way, are taking the teaching of the Master literally: It is possible to be "Christed," to be the child of God, the spiritual offspring, heir to all the spiritual riches. There have been people in all ages who have caught this vision; they have caught the vision of rising above human-hood. In the scriptures of the world, there are many accounts of religious leaders who were immaculately conceived. The Son of God can never be born or conceived in any other way except in the bosom of the Father: It is always an immaculate conception. These great spiritual lights died to their physical selfhood and were reborn of the Spirit. Gautama died to the name of Gautama in order to achieve the name of Buddha; Jesus died to the name of Jesus, the carpenter, to become the Christed one of God, the Son of God.

Everyone who dies to his humanhood is born into his spiritual nature and thereby loses that sense of humanhood which is born and can die. For that one there is neither birth nor death: There is only an eternal living. Whether or not that life remains visible to human beings is unimportant; whether or not you find a body to bury is unimportant; whether or not the body is left in a tomb or a casket is unimportant. In reality, there has never been a person with a physical body; there has never been a physical conception or a physical birth: These represent our finite sense of immaculate conception and the divinity of our being. We never lose our body: We lose our *sense* of the body. We lose our false concept of body and gain the true idea of body, in which there is neither sickness nor health: There is only immortality. To know Him aright is life eternal. There is no such thing as life eternal in mortality, so it must be life eternal in and as *immortality*—immortality even of the body, since our body, the very body, itself, is the temple of the living God.

At the spiritual level of life, we do not turn to God for supply or for health. At this point of life, we are likely to say to ourselves, "Why am I trying so desperately to demonstrate supply as if it were something good, when I have seen all the misery it has brought to so many? Why am I giving so much attention to the demonstration of health? I have seen many healthy people who are as unhappy as I am, or even more so." We begin to perceive that seeking health and seeking supply might have been legitimate at a certain stage of consciousness—so was playing with dolls when we were little children. However, just as it would not be considered desirable to be seen playing with dolls at the age of maturity, so in this spiritual age, we have no right to be playing with health or with supply: We should have outgrown that. A great deal of supply might be just as undesirable as too little supply; a great deal of health might lead us into more trouble than sickness. Our goal now is not supply, health, or companionship. Our goal now is a realization of Christhood.

When we give up the desire for supply, we shall have infinite riches even on the human plane. The minute we stop chasing supply, it will begin chasing us: It has never failed. The minute we give up the struggle for health, health will overtake us, but never as long as we are seeking it because we are searching for it as if it were somewhere ahead of us, outside of us, or beyond us; and it is not there. Health is not a condition of body; wealth is not a condition of the size of a bank account. Health and wealth are states of divine consciousness—omnipresent—just as omnipresent as integrity. If we should feel that it is necessary to give ourselves a treatment to become more honest, then we can also continue giving ourselves treatments for more health and more wealth; but if we believe that we have arrived at a state of integrity and honesty, then we must agree that we have also arrived at a state of health and wealth, because all these are inherent in divine consciousness.

Health belongs to God. Wholeness, completeness, perfection—these are not absent from God, the one Self, are they? Is there any other Self? Then why are we struggling for health and supply? They are not something separate and apart from us. Let them be revealed in us and through us just as our integrity is.

To many of us, it will prove to be a difficult step to say, "I am no longer trying to demonstrate health." I, myself, have been through the experience of having to give up the demonstration of supply at a time when I had no supply and the only human appearance was the need to demonstrate it, but I had to come to the realization: I have no supply to demonstrate, because the only supply that has any meaning to me is that which is already incorporated within me, the gift of God since "before Abraham was." Every time a temptation comes such as, "I need health; I need supply; I need something"; let us answer, "Why? To make me a richer mortal or a healthier mortal, or an older mortal on earth?" Let us be careful of that for which we pray: *We may get it.* "My grace is sufficient for thee"[10]—not more health, not more supply, but "My grace is sufficient for thee." We have been going to a spiritual God for a material good, and in doing that, we have been praying amiss.

Spiritual Living

Today we begin a new era in our experience, an era in which every day we bury some measure of our humanhood:

We are going to die every single day—some scrap of us is going to die—because we are going to deny ourselves. We are going to deny ourselves material good: We are no longer going to seek God in order to meet our needs. We are going to seek *God*—period. We are not going to seek God for the demonstration of health, wholeness, harmony, completeness. We are going to seek the demonstration of *God*—period. We are not going to seek the realization of God for some purpose. We are going to seek the realization of *God*—period. The minute we place that period after the word God, we find that the miracle begins. Every time we seek something *of* God, we are seeking a little more of mortality—of death. Every time we seek God, we are seeking life eternal.

There is a difference between human living and spiritual living. A human being is always seeking a person, place, thing, circumstance, or condition; and certainly, a human being is always seeking improvement. A human being is always seeking for more fish and bigger fish in his nets. Spiritual being says, "Leave your nets."

"If I leave my nets, how and what will I put my fish in?"

"Who says you are going to need fish?"

"But this is a fishing village; we live on fish—fish and bread."

"No, man lives not by bread alone, not even by fish, but by every word that proceedeth out of the mouth of God; so you do not need more fish, or bigger fish. You do not even need nets. You need no nets in the spiritual domain, none whatsoever."

In the spiritual kingdom, there is an entirely different mode of life, a mode of life which is represented by such promises as:

Eye hath not seen, nor ear heard, neither have entered into the heart of man, the things which God hath prepared for them that love him.[11]

I have meat to eat that ye know not of.[12]

Trust in the Lord, and do good; so shalt thou dwell in the land, and verily thou shalt be fed.[13]

If any man thirst, let him come unto me, and drink.[14]

Peace I leave with you, my peace I give unto you.[15]

The world gives us health and wealth, fame and fortune, but "*My* peace" is not the kind the world has to give. Jesus did not tell us what the nature of that peace was because to tell that to a human being would be nonsensical. The things of God are foolishness with man. When man is no longer man, God reveals what God has—a meat the world knows not of. That is a different kind of meat, a different kind of wine, a different kind of water, a different kind of bread. As human beings, we cannot understand this meat, water, or bread; but, as spiritual beings, we know what that spiritual food is. There is no need to tell the person of spiritual consciousness what he will find in spiritual living: He already knows the nature of the Christ in his life, but man whose breath is in his nostrils cannot understand the nature of spiritual living.

The question is frequently asked: "What do you find to take the place of the things you have given up? What do you find in the spiritual life?" We have no way of answering such questions because the things of God are foolishness with man. Actually we have given up nothing. True, we no longer have the outer form: The shadow has been superseded by the substance, and we now have the inner grace.

The next time you pray, watch and see if the form of your prayer or meditation has not changed. No matter what the form has been up until today, it must change from today on for this one reason: From today on, you will no longer seek the things that formerly you have been seeking. Heretofore, when you closed your eyes, there was in your mind a desire for health, harmony, wholeness, or completeness in some form; there was a seeking for some material form of good, and so the mind was kept busy trying to formulate the right kind of prayer or treatment. But now it is not important to find a method of prayer or treatment which will provide you with health or supply, companionship or home. Now the form of prayer or treatment must be one which will lead to the realization of God, the realization of the divine Presence, the realization of the divine Power, the realization of divine grace.

Watch the difference when you close your eyes now. You will find that the mind will not be unruly any more, once you have learned to sit down and say, "Well, at least, I have nothing to pray for, nothing to go to God for. I need no form of prayer or treatment, because there is nothing that I expect to get from this prayer or treatment. I can sit here at peace because there is nothing that I am seeking, nothing that I am desiring. I am not doing this for any thing; I am not seeking anything for myself, for my patients, for my students, or for my family. I am trusting the government of this universe to God and I do not have to tell Him anything or think any right thoughts. I do not even have to get a message from God; I do not have to have a vision. There is nothing that I want, so I am just going to sit here and be at peace—rest in Him and be still." When you turn in prayer with this understanding, you will find that you will be able to sit back in meditation, without a word or thought, and achieve that "click."

We need desire nothing. We have no need to pray for anything; we have no need to seek anything: There is no person, no place, no thing, no circumstance, or no condition for which we have to pray. Whatever there is, is in God's keeping, and it is well kept. We are dying daily to our human selfhood, and there is no use cluttering it up with more earthly things that will just make it more difficult for us to "die". All we are doing now is resting, and through divine grace, we shall find ourselves every minute of every hour of every day in possession of all spiritual wisdom.

"Not by might, nor by power, but by my Spirit, saith the Lord,"[16] not by our right thinking, not by our praying, not by our asking, "but by my Spirit, saith the Lord." And what are we doing when we close our eyes and ask and seek and affirm? We are trying to add to ourselves more humanly good conditions. From now on, we have none of these things to seek. From now on, we go to God for spiritual grace, for benediction, for blessing, for spiritual awareness, for rejoicing in the Spirit, for the riches of the Spirit, for the divine Comforter—the Christ. It is the function of the Christ to be our supplier, and this Christ functions on Its own level.

Why pray for the kind of bread that we do not need, for the meat for which we have no use? We have the Christ, the Comforter, that is come to be our meat—not to *give* us meat; but to *be* the meat, the wine, the water, the bread, the resurrection, and the life. Do we want something more than the Christ? Do we want something more than grace? Do we want something more than spiritual consciousness? Ah, yes, that is what we have been doing—wanting the Christ to give us bread, whereas the Christ *is* bread; praying the Christ to give us meat, whereas the Christ *is* the meat. Christ does not send meat to one, wine to another, and water to someone else. Christ's coming *is* the wine and the meat and the water and the bread. Is that clear?

There is no such thing as a demonstration of this and a demonstration of that. There is only one demonstration—the realization of the Christ. Then when the time comes for meat, there is meat; when the time comes for milk, the milk appears; when the time comes for wine, the wine is there. In every case, Christ is realized as omnipresent, and the realized Christ is our only need.

Never again must we seek bread, meat, wine, water, or truth. Seek the realization of the Christ, and let the Christ be that unto us which Its function really is. Christ is the Comforter: Shall we pray the Christ *for* the Comforter? Christ *is* the Comforter. There is no such thing as Christ *and;* there is no such thing as God *and.* When we seek God *for* something, we are building a false universe, one that has no existence. When we seek health and supply, we seek amiss. Christ *is* the health, the supply, the youth, the way, the truth, and the life.

Let us put no limit on God's capacity to reveal Itself. God's capacity is infinite. We limit that capacity by our present degree of receptivity, but in reality there is no limit to God's capacity to reveal Itself. All our prayers must now be for the realization of the Christ. Having Christ, we have meat, wine, water, bread, and life eternal—the way, the truth, and the life.

ACROSS THE DESK

As this *Letter* is being written, students are beginning to arrive from the United States and Canada for the August class work. Next week Australia, England, and South America will be represented here, also. It is an inspiration to think that there are approximately a hundred students, each sufficiently serious to be willing to make an expenditure of at least one thousand dollars, and in some cases considerably more than that, in order to come to Hawaii for these Infinite Way Closed Classes. Only the increased harmony and inner peace of the student could bring this to pass. It is a testimony as to what can be attained by the serious study and practice of The Infinite Way.

The example of Students coming from all over the world to attend these classes should inspire all our other students to be more earnest in their study and meditations. There is but one spiritual law on this subject: "To him that hath shall be given."[17] It is impossible to give more of healing or other forms of harmony than the student himself can put into the activity.

This brings into thought the age-old question: Why do some people receive quick and complete healing, comfort, peace, and supply, while others receive these fruits of the Spirit but slowly, and still others not at all? I doubt that anyone has the full and complete answer to this question. Sometimes I have felt that the slowness of healing—or absence of it—might be due in part to the fact that students or patients do not understand the principles of healing and, therefore, cannot adjust their consciousness to the spiritual experience. This is not entirely the fault of the student. It is true that if a student truly dedicated himself to The Infinite Way writings, enough of a healing consciousness would evolve to enable him to be healed of anything and even to begin to do some healing work himself. But the average person is not enough of a student to dedicate himself to such a work.

For the sake of helping students more readily and quickly to grasp the healing principles of The Infinite Way, and thereby raise consciousness to the level of accepting and experiencing more healing, and even doing some healing work themselves, our 1957 June, July, and August *Letters* have been written to fill this need. A few months of really diligent study and practice of these three *Letters* could work miracles in the students' experience. I shall be interested to hear of the effect of these *Letters* on the lives of our students. A further help is to be found in the compilation in book form of *The Infinite Way Letters of* 1954, 1955, and 1956. These *Letters* are links in our chain of student-teacher relationship.

Only those, however, who have devoted hours of study to the previous *Letters* will be able to grasp this September *Letter* with any degree of understanding. In it, you have a foretaste of what lies ahead of you in the mystical experience which is the goal of The Infinite Way.

To *live* The Infinite Way is to contemplate God and the ways of the Spirit, and by meditation to enter into actual communion with God. The ability to commune with God is the great step necessary to the attainment of our goal—conscious union with God. It is only in communion with God and the attainment of conscious oneness that we rise above all forms of healing into a continuous life of the Spirit where there is neither good nor evil, health nor disease, but only the experience of eternal life.

Please remember, students, we are but children in Christ. Let us be patient with each other and always helpful. Let none of us claim the realized Christ in its fulness, but, knowing that it has been and can be attained, let us dedicate ourselves to this attainment. Let us not be satisfied with a sufficiency of supply or of physical health: These are but steps leading to the grand attainment. We are companions and helpers to each other on the path. We welcome those who are on the way of God-realization to unite with us in prayer and communion, regardless of their particular path. We seek no memberships—no followers. We seek only to share the light with all who desire it.

It is necessary that you understand the healing principles of The Infinite Way thoroughly so that you can be readily healed of all human discords. Know the principles so thoroughly that you can explain them to seekers and be the instrument for the healing of those who seek healing. Your moments and hours *of understanding prayer* are needed to support The Infinite Way activities around the clock and around the world and, even more important, to uphold the arms of our fellow-workers around the world.

If you love The Infinite Way this much, God will show you what is required of you to further the activity of carrying the Word to human awareness.

✤ 10 ✤

OCTOBER

Bear Witness

For thou shalt be his witness unto all men of what thou hast seen and heard.

Acts 22:15

There was a man sent from God, whose name was John. The same came for a witness, to bear witness of the Light, that all men through him might believe. He was not that Light, but was sent to bear witness of that Light.

John 1:6–8

We speak what we do know, and testify that we have seen.

John 3:11

If I bear witness of myself, my witness is not true.

John 5:31

And we are his witnesses of these things.

Acts 5:32

Ye are my witnesses, saith the Lord, and my servant whom I have chosen; that we may know and believe me, and understand that I am he: before me there was no God formed, neither shall there be after me.

Isaiah 43:10

In a courtroom, a witness mounts the witness stand, not to *interpret* his observations, but simply to tell *what* he has seen. A witness bears witness to that which he has seen take place. At no point should a witness say, "I brought this about; I did this; or I helped this"; but rather, "This is what I saw, and I am repeating it as I saw it." That is what the Master meant by bearing witness to God. The Master bore witness to God's power. He claimed no power for himself, "I can of mine own self do nothing ...[1] the Father that dwelleth in me, he doeth the works,"[2] that is, "I bear witness to that which I see the Father do."

In The Infinite Way, we do not *use* God. Instead we sit in quietness and stillness, *watching God do the work*. Then we can say, "I witnessed a healing; I witnessed the activity of God in human affairs; I did not do it; I had no part in it, but I bore witness to God performing His work."

Let us suppose that a call for help comes to us. Can I give the help or can you give it? Those of us who have been the instruments for healing know the answer to that question: No human being can give that help. If God does not answer the call, it will not be answered. But you say, "God is not answering all the calls that go out to Him for help. The hospitals are filled with diseased bodies and the mental institutions with the broken in spirit; the battlefields are covered with the maimed and the dead. God is not responding to all these calls for help." That is true because God cannot answer on earth. God can only answer as He finds entrance through consciousness, through a consciousness completely devoid of ego, a consciousness so imbued with the understanding that God is, that the one thus imbued is willing to sit back in complete surrender: "Father, this is your universe. Take over."

God cannot appear on earth except through consciousness; God cannot appear on earth except *as* consciousness, not as the human, thinking, reasoning consciousness, but as the consciousness which is still. This does not eliminate the thinking, reasoning mind. Rather does that mind become an instrument used by the still small voice which is consciousness or God.

In other words, if I am a state of silent receptivity, what I am writing is being imparted to me through the Spirit; then, through the activity of the mind, it can be voiced; and through your mind, it can enter your consciousness. The human mind or human consciousness is not erased; thinking or reasoning is not stopped, but these are not accepted as God: They are looked upon as instruments through which God works. God works independently of any human help; God needs no human aid; God cannot be influenced by a human being—not even a human being's desire to save life.

Spiritual Attunement

As human beings, we have no control over the bodies of other people; we cannot reduce fevers or remove lumps. We have no control over the business of other people; we cannot make people more intelligent in the operation of their business nor can we make them more loving in their business transactions: We have no such power over their business. But if we are willing to admit that there is a God, which operates through the stillness of our thinking, reasoning mind, then we can let that God be released through us so that It will act to make the inadequate intelligence, adequate; It will make the unloving, loving; It can make the ungrateful, grateful; It can make the unthinking, thinking, rational beings; It will make the diseased thought, healthy thought; It will make the diseased body, the diseased business, and the diseased profession, healthy. This It will do, and we can bear witness to that fact. We can bear witness to the power of Spirit in human affairs. We cannot operate It; we cannot make It do our will; we cannot send It out to make It heal those we should like to see healed. No, we cannot do any of these things, but if we can be still, the activity of God will find outlet through us and touch the receptive and responsive thought. Even God cannot work through those who are unreceptive and unresponsive; there has to be a receptivity and a responsiveness through which God can operate.

The more spiritual our consciousness is, the more clearly will the answers come through from God. That is the reason why we cannot teach these principles to students in six, eight, or ten easy lessons. If they, themselves, have not relinquished their fear, hate, or love of the evil *and* the good of the human world, the presence, the activity, and the power of God cannot come through. However, if we have attuned our thought to God's purpose through years of study of the Bible and other spiritual literature, in that degree will our consciousness be so illumined that when we sit down for the solution of a problem, it will come through.

I know absolutely nothing of what is underneath the hood of an automobile. I have never had any occasion to look to find out and still less curiosity, so that I can truthfully tell you that I would not know a carburetor from a generator. Twice, however, I have had the experience of having the motor of my automobile stop dead in traffic. Of course, there are any number of human solutions to such a problem. For example, I could have been towed into the nearest garage or I could have secured the services of a mechanic to make the necessary repairs. But in both cases, these situations did not lend themselves to either of these solutions. So, instead, I got out and lifted the hood of the automobile. From a human standpoint, certainly there could not have been any more foolish thing in the world for me to do than that because I did not know what to look for after it was open. Nevertheless, I did just that; I opened the hood, and on both occasions the same thing happened. After a rather desultory inspection of the mass of paraphernalia under the hood, I saw a loose wire which I picked up in my hand, and then looking around I noticed a gadget which was similar to others with wires hooked to them, but inasmuch as this one had no wire connected to it, I proceeded to fasten the loose wire to it, got in my car, and drove away.

That was spiritual attunement because there was no human knowledge involved in the operation—none whatsoever. I looked under the hood, knowing when I did so that I had no idea what I was looking for, and then something greater than myself said, "There it is, right there." That is an example of the principle of our work in The Infinite Way—bearing witness to the activity of God.

Bear Witness to God in Action

Whenever a problem is presented to me by one of our students, my own procedure is to be a witness, to bear witness to the activity of God—to sit still long enough for the Presence to announce Itself. Then I drop it. If something points out the next step the student should take, or if that something removes a fever or a lump, I have merely borne witness to the activity of Spirit. When the Spirit announces Itself within, something happens not only to the physical body, but many times the whole life of those who touch an illumined consciousness takes on a different direction, and new worlds are opened up. If we are still enough, the Spirit comes through and works these miracles. Then we can say, "I bore witness to the activity of the Spirit; the Spirit was operating; the Spirit was on the field."

Bear witness to God in action. Watch the activity of God with such certainty and detachment that you could go on a witness stand and say, "I saw God in action." Any success in our work is not the miracle-working power of any man; it is the ability to stand a few inches to the side of ourselves and watch God come through. That is the miracle of this work. It is the very thing the Master must have meant when he said, "Why callest thou me good? ...[3] I can of mine own self do nothing ...[4] The Father that dwelleth in me, he doeth the works.[5] ... I bear witness ... My Father worketh hitherto and I work."[6] The meaning of these statements will become very clear, if only we remember that never did Jesus multiply loaves and fishes. The Bible says he looked up. That is the answer: He looked up and let the Father perform the miracle; he let the Father multiply the loaves and fishes.

There is a Father, whether you call It Father, Father-Mother, the Christ, or God. These terms have little or no meaning. The words, themselves, are not important; use any word that has meaning for you. For me the miracle-working word in my consciousness is the Christ. The Christ has been the central theme of my revelation. The Christ is that which has real meaning to me, and when I say, "Live through the Christ and in the Christ," I have an absolute conviction that I am speaking of a Presence, a Power, a Spirit, a Substance, an Activity that is much more real than electricity. As a matter of fact, it could wipe out electricity, if there were any reason for so doing—I have seen It wipe out the effects of electricity many times.

There is a Something which you may call the Christ, Tao, Brahm, God, or the Infinite Invisible. It makes no difference what you call It as long as in your consciousness there is that unswerving conviction that you are imbued and endowed with that Something, with an Infinity, an Omnipresence, an Omniscience, an Omnipotence which cannot be manipulated or influenced. The best way to be an instrument for It is to follow The Infinite Way teaching of being a beholder. Sit quietly in the realization: "Thank you, Father; I am beginning with the understanding that I can of mine own self do nothing; and even if I could, I would not know what to do, or how to do it."

Be a Beholder of the Divine Flow

Develop for yourself a type of meditation which ultimately will enable you to relax as if you were resting on a cloud, until the Spirit flows out from you. Then you are a witness, a beholder of that divine flow. You may not see anything; you may not even feel anything, but you will have an awareness of It, and then It will be for you the Presence that goes before you to make the crooked places straight. It will put the crops in the ground before the seed; It will bring gold out of the fish's mouth; It will bring manna from the sky and water from the rocks. *You* will not do this; *you* will never be a miracle-worker, but you will be a beholder of more miracles than any group of people on earth has ever witnessed. You will behold substance being renewed, the sick being healed, the dead coming to life, and the lost years of the locusts being restored. You will bear witness to all that by being a beholder—just by stepping aside to watch It as It flows.

Bear witness to God in action: Do not try to make God act; do not try to bring God to the scene; do not try to use God; do not try to influence God; do not try to use truth in any way or for any purpose. Bear witness to Its omnipresence; bear witness to Its omnipotence, Its omniscience; be a beholder of It in action. The world, looking on, will marvel and say of you as it said of Jesus, "It was never so seen in Israel."[7] This it said even though Jesus denied his ability as a man to do these mighty works. So they will say of you, "You are healing the sick. You are raising the dead; you are a wonder-worker."

And you will be saying to yourself, "Oh, foolish person, can't you see? Can't you see that there is a God? All that I can do is to be silent in His presence. How can I bear witness to God except in silence?" When the senses are still, God is on the field. In the moment that ye think not, the bridegroom cometh—in the moment that ye think not. That has been misinterpreted, but it means just what it says, "In such an hour as ye *think* not."[8] When you are still and when you are silent, then the flow begins. Nobody can heal; nobody can save; nobody can regenerate: God is, and only God is.

Our function in life is to be a witness to God in action, disregarding and looking through every appearance. No matter what the condition may appear to be, through this inner vision, we bear witness to the omnipresence of the Christ which is the activity of God in human consciousness.

The world has not yet discovered the illusory nature of error, and therefore, it believes that if you are sinning, you are the one who has to be reformed; if you are subject to false appetites, it is you who have to be treated, reformed, corrected, or improved; if you are sick, it is you who need healing; if you are poor, it is undoubtedly something for which, inwardly, you are responsible or of which you are a victim. In other words, the word "you" is the devil, because the world believes that if you are sinful, it is your fault; if you are poor, it is usually your fault—even though you may have had nothing to do with being poor. If you are sick, it is because of something you did—you contracted the disease by sitting in a draft, by getting in the way of some germ or other, by living in the wrong climate, or by eating the wrong food.

All religions teach: God is all; God is everywhere equally present; God is perfect; God is love; God governs, guides, and directs. While admitting these truths in theory, few followers of religious teachings seriously attempt to practice these basic tenets of their faith because the majority of them believe not only in the power of good, but in the power of evil: They accept two powers. In the first place, they ascribe goodness to you as a person, and humanly, you have no goodness: Humanly, you are not good; humanly, you are not spiritual; humanly, you are not perfect; humanly, you are not harmonious. Instead of bearing witness to your goodness, your perfection, and your spirituality, as is done in many metaphysical teachings, if you will bear witness to God in action, you will immediately bring about a change of some kind. You will bring about a change for good in your experience the very moment that you disclaim qualities of goodness as your personal possession and declare, "Do not call me good; do not call me spiritual; do not call me anything. God is the only good; God is the only activity of good; God is the only law of good; God is the only cause; and God is the only effect. There is no 'I,' 'me,' or 'mine'; there is only God—God Itself within Itself, expressing Itself unto Itself. God is the all in all." When you bear witness to God as the life of individual being, God as the mind of individual being, the law, cause, and effect of individual being, you have begun your spiritual unfoldment.

As long as you are using words like "he," "she," and "it," or "I," "me," and "mine," you are trying to spiritualize form;

you are trying to spiritualize the shadow of life. This is just as incorrect as is the religious doctrine which teaches that we human beings are miserable sinners, not fit to approach the hem of the Robe. Both of these approaches are wrong because God alone is good and beside God there is none other. There is no "I," "he," "she," or "it"; that which appears to us as "I," "he," "she," or "it" is God; and if only you can see with spiritual vision, you will behold God in action. You will see that it is God in manifestation—God Itself. When you see God instead of an "it," "he," or "she," then the "it," "he," or "she" begins to take on more nearly the likeness of God-being.

Instead of declaring any virtue for yourself or for others, recognize all virtue as of God:

God alone is the light of the day. God alone is the brightness of the night. God alone is the law of growth, progress, or unfoldment. God alone is the source of all being. God alone is the Soul, the purity, and the perfection of all being.

That is bearing witness to God in action—God omnipresent, God omnipotent, God omniscient, God as all in all. You will never succeed in this practice as long as you are dealing with persons. You only succeed in proportion as you bear witness to God in action and realize God: God alone is being; God is eternal being; God is immortal being, perfect and harmonious; God is the essence of all life.

Bear Witness to the Illusory Nature of Error

Bearing witness to God in action will begin to bring changes in your experience, but this one step, in and of itself, will not bring the final and complete demonstration of harmony or of spiritual power in your life. It is necessary not merely to bear witness to God in action, but to bear witness to the illusory nature of error in order to bring the final demonstration of harmony into your experience. Just as you are not good, so you are not evil. You are not responsible for the ills you are experiencing: You are not a sinner; you are not the one who is poor; you are not the one who contracts a disease. Your wrong thinking did not cause your problems, and your right thinking will not cure them.

There is only one thing that will bring an end to the discords and inharmonies of individual experience, and that is an understanding of the truth. The first point in this understanding is not to call anyone good because there is but one good; there is but one life; there is but one mind, one Soul, one law, one cause, one being, and one effect. The other and equally important part of the understanding of truth is not to call anyone evil because a person has no more to do with the evil appearance than he has to do with its opposite, the good appearance. When we appear to be good, it is the activity of God operating through us. When we appear to be evil, it is the activity of material sense which is only a sense of separation from God.

For example, if you saw a thief whom you wanted to help, you would not accept into your consciousness a person needing to be healed of dishonesty: You would separate the dishonesty from the person and you would recognize this as a universal belief in a selfhood apart from God, a universal belief in lack and limitation, or a universal belief in the possibility that someone can get good from another, all of which beliefs are without power. In other words, whatever form the error assumes, it is not an error belonging to any person: It is simply a universal belief. Never forget that error is nothing but a universal belief.

Error Is Not Personal
to the Individual

When an individual comes to us for help, the first thing that we must do is to bear witness to God in action. Within ourselves, we bear witness to the realization that right here, invisible, is the Christ. The activity of the Christ, or the Spirit of God, is on the field, even though appearances testify otherwise. Then what about this appearance that is being presented to us? It is the one illusion, the universal belief of a separation from good; it is the universal belief of a law apart from God.

The very moment that you stop personalizing good, you start the flow of blessing; the moment that you stop personalizing evil, you complete the picture. You begin to nullify the evil the very moment that you can look at it, perhaps expressing in the form of a Judas Iscariot, and say, "This man, Judas, is not a sinner. Father, forgive him; he knows not what he does. This is only a sense of a selfhood apart from God and, as such, it is neither a presence nor a power; it has no one in whom or through whom to operate."

First bear witness, regardless of appearances, to God in action:

God is the life of this individual, the mind, the Soul, and the Spirit. God is the only law operating in and through and as this individual. God is the only being; God is the only cause; God is the only effect. This is a spiritual universe, the product of a spiritual, creative law and of spiritual being.

Thus, you are bearing witness to God in action. But you say, "What of this sin or this evil that I am beholding?" Yes, what of it? We are not going to deny what we are seeing, but we are going to recognize that it is no part of the individual. We are going to accept it only as a universal belief of a selfhood apart from God which has nothing to do with this individual.

An example of the universal nature of the beliefs which attach themselves to us is found in observing recurring behavior patterns in children at certain age levels. All children are very much alike at the same age, and most of them behave in much the same manner. They do the same delightfully amusing things and they do the same annoying things. A two-year-old child is two years old, and you cannot make him anything else. He will be troublesome at times, and at other times, he will be angelic. And the reason? It is not the child at all; it is being two years of age.

When a child is thirteen years of age, he will act like thirteen years. Watch one child of thirteen and you have watched almost all children at thirteen. The same mischief one gets into the others get into. Of course, there may be some slight differences because all tastes are not alike. One will be mischievous in one way and another in another way; one will be good in one way and another in another way. But on the whole, if you look at ten-year-old children, at thirteen-year-old children, or at sixteen-year-old children, you will have to admit that they have all come out of practically the same mold. That is as close to being universally true as almost anything can be. Why? Because the children themselves have nothing to do with it; they are responding to the human belief about them at that particular age. It is a universal belief that adolescents are impertinent and disobedient and believe that their parents do not know anything. That latter belief is so universal that we have the saying: "At twenty, I knew that I knew everything that was to be known in the world. At thirty, I began to suspect that perhaps I did not know it all, and at forty, I knew that it was my parents who knew it all."

Everyone goes through these beliefs and responds to the same type of thing in much the same way because it is a response to a universal belief. Handle error as a universal claim instead of as your error or mine. Instead of fastening some form of error on a person by believing that this person is obstinate, this person is dictatorial, this one is dishonest, and this one immoral, or this person is so and so, ignore the appearance presented by the person. Do not ignore the claim. Never ignore the claim. Ignore the person and handle the claim by realizing that the claim is not personal; it has nothing to do with the person involved. It is a universal sense of a selfhood apart from God and a universal sense of a law apart from God.

If you were dealing with the universal belief in a law of infection or a law of contagion, you would not blame your patient for it. If God is law and God is infinite, there can be no law of disease, no law of infection, and no law of contagion. Such so-called laws are only universal beliefs. Would you blame a tiny child for contracting an infectious, contagious disease? The child had nothing to do with it; the child is the innocent victim of a universal belief just as is the adult. This is true regardless of the name or nature or depth or degree of the sin or disease.

Through the realization that age has nothing to do with a person, there has been some remarkable work done among people who are under the claim of old age. Since the only person is God appearing as individual being, we are all the same age as God. No person, therefore, can be older than another person because God is infinite person. But the universal belief in a life and a selfhood apart from God, the universal belief in a law of the deterioration of matter, and in the law of diminishing returns is the problem. Recognize that there is neither youth nor age; there is only God.

Bear Witness to God as Individual Being

Regardless of what condition you see on earth, bear witness to God in action. Regardless of what condition you see in a person, bear witness to the truth that God is individual being. God constitutes all there is to this being; God is the creative principle; God is the maintaining and sustaining influence. As you drive your car or as you walk through the crowded city streets, bear witness to God in action. Bear witness to the fact that here indeed is the very Christ.

Common sense says to you, "Oh, but what I am looking at does not look like the Christ. What I am seeing, the horrors I am witnessing—surely these things are not the Christ in action." It is at this point that it is necessary to take the second step and bear witness to the illusory nature of error: "No, I am seeing the effects of a universal sense of a selfhood apart from God. I am seeing the effects of a universal belief in a law or activity or cause apart from God. Such beliefs, being only beliefs, are not power. They do not have the activity of God behind them; they do not have the law of God to support them or uphold them or sustain them. I see them for what they are—a belief in a selfhood apart from God, or a belief in a medical or theological law, or a belief in a substance or activity apart from God."

There is an invisible Presence and Power in the universe, the Infinite Invisible. The Infinite Invisible appears as the visible. This Infinite Invisible is the law unto that which is visible; the Infinite Invisible is the essence and the activity of the visible. We look only to the Infinite Invisible for our good and for the good of the universe—not to anyone or to anything. In such reliance, the "anyone" or "anything" in the visible becomes the instrument through which the Invisible operates. The Infinite Invisible can so purify us that never again would we injure each other; never again would we be unjust, unkind, or untrue to each other; never would we be negative in any way, shape, manner, or form to each other.

Let us catch the vision: Behold God in action, but also behold any and every form of error as universal belief. There is only God, but God appears on earth as man; God is expressed as individual being. God is the substance, the cause, and the law unto all being. Evil does not exist as a cause *in* a person; evil does not exist *as* a person: Evil is a state of illusion. Let us bear witness to God in action and then bear witness to the universal nature of evil as illusion, not as power. There is but one power—God; there is but one good—God.

Good can only be brought into your experience and the experience of others in proportion as there is an individual so unselfed as to be willing to bear witness to God in action. The Hebrews might still be slaves under Pharaoh had there not been a Moses with a good helper like Aaron. Moses knew that he was slow of speech, which we might interpret to mean that he recognized that while he did not know enough to lead the Hebrews out of Egypt, he was willing to be obedient to God and let God speak through him while he kept silent. Day after day, Jesus was willing to repeat, "I can of mine own self do nothing."[9] He was satisfied to sit with eyes closed and let the Father within him do the works.

There are no modern practitioners or teachers capable of healing your ills or bringing peace on earth, but there are many dedicated mystics, spiritual teachers, writers, and practitioners who are willing to sit in the silence, and behold the presence and power of God as It operates in human affairs.

Remember, there must be a Moses or a Jesus, or there must be a you or a me; there must be an individual willing to be silent and bear witness to God acting through his consciousness to change your life and the events of the world.

In your turn, as an Infinite Way student, you must be one of those willing to acknowledge that you are slow of speech, that you have insufficient understanding, and that you humanly, of yourself, have no spiritual power. Then, in this denial of self, be still and let the still small voice utter Truth through you.

> The voice of the Lord is powerful; the voice of the Lord is full of majesty.
>
> The voice of the Lord breaketh the cedars; yea, the Lord breaketh the cedars of Lebanon. ...
>
> The voice of the Lord divideth the flames of fire.
>
> The voice of the Lord shaketh the wilderness ...
>
> The voice of the Lord maketh the hinds to calve, and discovereth the forests: and in his temple doth every one speak of his glory. ...
>
> The Lord will give strength unto his people; the Lord will bless his people with peace.[10]

Often our students write telling me of their discouragement and frustration because they do not think they are developing fast enough spiritually or because they do not have sufficient spiritual understanding. My rebuke to these students is sometimes severe. I cannot help but wonder if they are expecting to be greater than Moses, Jesus, or John. In fact, every true mystic has been acutely aware of his own inadequacy and has gloried in it rather than deplored it.

Throughout The Infinite Way writings, you will find how often I have written that I do not know how to heal. Perhaps you think this is just false modesty, or that I am only pretending to be modest. Nothing could be further from the truth. Frankly, I do not know how to heal a simple headache or a simple cold, nor how to bring peace, prosperity, or happiness into the lives of our students. But, armed with the conviction that human knowledge is not spiritual power, I am willing to sit in meditation from ten to twenty times every day to contemplate God and the things of God—sometimes to enter into actual communion with God—and then wait in stillness for the presence and power of God to utter Itself within me, or within you, while I sit quietly, behold, and then later bear witness to the greater harmonies that appear in the lives of our students. There *is* a Spirit in man, but we have to be still and let It express Itself while we behold It at work and then bear witness to Its fruitage.

I hope that you do not think that Joel is writing this message for you. No, Joel is sitting in his office; his eyes are looking upward to the hills from whence cometh our help, and there is a kind of vacuum in him as he sits watching the trees and flowers, and hears the birds singing. This message is coming through him while he marvels that God's grace permits him to be the instrument through which you will receive it. If Joel were not sitting here in this listening attitude, either the world would never receive this message or someone other than Joel would have to be giving it out, because the activity of God can only reach the earth through an individual, an individual who is silent and receptive. You must be that person for your family, for your patients, for your students, or for those who come to you for spiritual help.

To Our More Serious Students

We are in the midst of an experience which may transform the nature of our work and the world's demonstration of spiritual healing.

We know that a spiritual healing cannot be achieved by reading a book or a dozen books, or taking a course of lessons. These are but steps leading to that moment when your consciousness drops its material faiths and becomes imbued with spiritual light. Those who through the years have been faithful and diligent in the study and practice of metaphysical or spiritual truth have developed a healing consciousness and helped the world come this far in spiritual evolution. However, we now have in the June through October 1957 *Letters* a course of instruction in healing principles which, if faithfully and persistently studied and practiced over a period of time, not only will evolve a healing consciousness for you—enabling you better to heal and to be healed—but you will, by your increased healings, show all metaphysicians that through the principles given in these *Letters* and amplified in all our writings that they too can increase their healing consciousness.

Only if Infinite Way students become known as good healers and teachers, will other metaphysicians come to realize the value of these principles and be led to adopt them into their lives and practice. Remember always that we are not seeking members or followers: Our aim is to make spiritual healing principles available to everyone in the metaphysical and orthodox church movements. Our hope is that all the world may live and heal by spiritual principles and that we may be an instrument through which this may come about.

Already the healings, which have taken place through the principles taught in The Infinite Way writings, have carried this message around the world. Now that the healing principles are embodied in a few *Letters*, it will be possible for earnest students to go far in this direction—and by their works and example carry these principles to all who seek healing, or seek to be healers.

But do not be fooled by the simplicity or brevity of the June through October *Letters*. They must be studied and practiced while a healing consciousness is evolving.

Blessed are you, if now *knowing,* you follow through and do.

Across the Desk

Looking at the human scene, we see continual strife and struggle—good battling evil, health trying to conquer disease, virtue contending against vice, abundance racing to keep a step ahead of lack, war and peace see-sawing constantly, and birth and death occupying the same pages of the papers.

When muskets were invented, the bow-and-arrow nations were conquered, only to be conquered in turn when rifles came into being. When the power of a torpedo launched from a submarine became more potent than the power of guns or cannon on ships, the submarine defeated the world's largest navies. The airplane has overcome land armies, and the newest weapon, atomic power, has filled the whole world with fear. Medicine and surgery continue their warfare with disease. Education valiantly wages its battle with ignorance, superstition, and fear. We can sum it all up in one phrase—the struggle for survival. Noting how one power always overcomes a lesser power, only in its turn to be overcome by a still greater power, we may well ask: Where will all this end? Can this struggle continue forever with one ogre devouring another? Looking at the scene from a material standpoint, the answer to the problem of survival is always found in the discovery of a still greater power than that which is already known.

Everywhere in the world, people are recognizing that there must come an end to this eternal warfare of mind and matter and that some other solution must be found. In The Infinite Way, we believe that we have found the solution to life's problems and to a way of harmonious living—a way *not based on power.* An understanding of this way begins to dissolve our personal problems, brings about more harmonious family, business, and social relationships, and includes in this harmony all those who are or who become a part of our consciousness. Eventually, this way will be the way of all mankind and the word "power" will then be used merely in measuring the forces of electricity or atomic energy.

In August, approximately one hundred students assembled here in Hawaii, students who came from all parts of the mainland—from the Atlantic to the Pacific Coast—from Canada, England, Australia, and South America. One hotel in Honolulu reserved all its accommodations for Infinite Way students, and another half dozen hotels housed others, while a few were guests in the homes of friends. These students came from these great distances at great expense to attend the Halekou Closed Classes. And why did they come? If each student who came had asked himself or herself that question, perhaps not one of them would have been able to give a "sensible" or a "reasonable" answer. There is no answer in materialism, because materialism can only evaluate an experience in terms of material gain, and there was no possible hope of any material or tangible gain. Yet these students came; they were here; and they were drawn here without any slightest urging—absolutely no power of any kind was utilized to draw them here.

Our students have learned from my writings and from their own experience that God constitutes individual being, and therefore each one is secure in his own spiritual integrity, one with his Source. Each one represents God fulfilling Itself. Each is fed by the inner meat, wine, bread, and water within his own Self. Each draws life, sustenance, and wisdom from the springs of living water within his own being. Each draws inspiration from the hills from whence cometh our help—that high consciousness which has evolved through unselfed living, giving, and sharing. Our students have learned that neither health, harmony, nor supply can be received, but these can be given forth from that which is within each one of them.

No power drew these students from 2,500 to 9,000 miles to be here—no promises, no suggestions, no hopes of gain, not even the expectancy of learning of greater powers. In this grand experience you may, with spiritual discernment, glimpse the principles of The Infinite Way. It may help you to understand the passage which appears on the opening page of all our writings:

> Illumination dissolves all material ties and binds men together with the golden chains of spiritual understanding; it acknowledges only the leadership of the Christ; it has no ritual or rule but the divine, impersonal universal Love; no other worship than the inner Flame that is ever lit at the shrine of Spirit. This union is the free state of spiritual brotherhood. The only restraint is the discipline of Soul, therefore we know liberty without license; we are a united universe without physical limits; a divine service to God without ceremony or creed.[11]

If you can only dimly perceive the nature of this passage, you will understand the miracle that drew those students here and that has also drawn such groups together in Seattle, Portland, Chicago, New York, London, Amsterdam, South Africa, Australia, and other places. To discern this is to understand the nature of The Infinite Way and its mode of revealing Omnipresence. Is there more than this? Ponder and meditate.

When you are faced with some of the problems of "this world," will you not remember that the answer does not lie in using some power—not even some power of God—to overcome or destroy anything? Will you not see that only in "this world" does one power strive with another, but in "My kingdom" there are no powers.

❖ 11 ❖

GRATITUDE

FEW PEOPLE UNDERSTAND the nature of gratitude. Just what is gratitude? Are human beings capable of gratitude? Actually, we should not expect gratitude from a person, and if we do expect it, we shall be disappointed because gratitude is beyond the capacity of a human being.

Many people believe that money and gratitude are synonymous, but in reality, they have no relationship to each other. There are times when money can be a symbol of gratitude, but it is a mistake to tie them together because gratitude goes far beyond money. For example, if we should ask a practitioner for help for a headache and attempted to express our gratitude in a monetary form, we might well believe that a nominal payment would be a sufficient expression of gratitude; but on the other hand, if we were healed of a cancer, we might feel that even if we took our last dollar and ran into debt besides, it would be a very small token of gratitude for such a healing. In both cases, we would be wrong, because gratitude for spiritual healing has no relationship at all to what has been healed.

Spiritual healing can only come through a realization of God. It can only take place when an individual has so dedicated himself to spiritual living that he becomes a transparency through which God can act; and when the Spirit of God flows through an individual, that Spirit of God can heal the headache or the cancer. There should be no difference in the degree of gratitude in either case because our gratitude should not be merely for the healing of a headache or for the healing of a cancer. No, we should be grateful because we have been privileged to be a living witness to the fact that God is as available on earth today as He was two thousand years ago. How, then, can we be more grateful for the presence of God in one case than in another?

The world at large does not have access to God because it has cut itself off from contact with God. Many people believe that if they go to church on Sunday or contribute to the poor-box, they are doing their duty to God. It is true that these activities, if engaged in with devotion and dedication, may be an expression of our love for God. But our relationship to God is something deeper than that; it must be a relationship of constant communion, with our lives lived in God.

As students on the way, let us learn to be grateful, not for a healing, not for supply, not for harmony in one form or another; but let us learn to be grateful for the realization of God's presence. Let us be grateful that the omnipresence of God is our safety and security, our peace on earth. Let us learn to abide in the realization that God's presence is our fortress, our high tower, and our eternal dwelling place.

Gratitude for the Realization of the Spirit

When we learn to express gratitude for any teaching, teacher, or practitioner, or any individual experience that brings God's presence to our mind or body, then we are properly expressing gratitude. When we awaken in the morning and behold nature in any of its varied forms of beauty, we should remember that it is the activity of God that is responsible for that manifestation. The activity of God is responsible for every form of good we behold. If we observe the blossoming fruit trees or if we note the fruitage itself, remember that it is not the fruit; it is the Spirit, or a law of nature, which brought forth that fruitage, and it is that Spirit for which we should be grateful. Then we can use our fruit; then we can use our food or our money, letting them come and letting them go, because behind these is the Spirit which produced them. When our gratitude is for the Spirit that *produces* our healings or our supply, when our gratitude is for the *Spirit* that holds us in Its arms—the everlasting arms underneath us, in us, beneath us, above us, permeating us—when our gratitude is for that Spirit of God, then we are being truly grateful.

Such gratitude may have nothing to do with money, and yet at other times, it may direct us to give money, share money, or spend money. Words, in and of themselves, are often empty and meaningless. A perfunctory "thank you" can never be an adequate expression of gratitude. True gratitude often carries with it some tangible evidence of its sincerity, either in the form of money or service because gratitude, like love, is not an abstraction.

The important point to remember is to be grateful *not* for any form of good but for the Spirit which underlies that form, the Spirit which produces that form. We learn to be just as grateful when we witness the healing of a headache, indigestion, or a corn as we would be for the healing of cancer, consumption, or polio. Our response will always be, "What is the difference? What *difference* is there between the two?" We understand why the Master could walk up to the leper and touch the leprosy, or why he could say to the woman taken in adultery, "Neither do I condemn thee."[1] Whether a large or a small offense, a serious disease or a minor ailment, it was all the same to Jesus: These were but a sense of separation from God; Therefore his healings were quick and easy, whether it was leprosy, consumption, the impotent man sitting at the pool, the crippled man, or whether it was the young boy who was a corpse, or Peter's mother-in-law. The *forms* of disease and the *forms* of sin meant nothing to him. He knew that the healing power was the Spirit of God, and that if the Spirit of God could be brought to the case, it made no difference what degree of error was presented.

Even the magnitude of the demand to feed the multitudes with only a few loaves and fishes did not disturb or frighten him. He knew that men are not fed by bread alone but by the Spirit of God, and when the Spirit of God is present, there is no limit to supply. If you have realized that Spirit of God, you will not have to be concerned about whether you have the responsibility of caring for one person or are required to take on the obligation of a whole family or community. If you try to provide for them through "bread alone," then you will have your worries; but if you understand that you are feeding, supporting, supplying, and healing through the Spirit of God, the numbers or the amount of money involved will be of no concern to you. It may be fifty dollars or fifty thousand dollars, five people or five thousand. The number or amount will mean *nothing* in your experience because within you will be the recognition, "Numbers are of no interest to me. If I have the Spirit of God, it is complete; if I do not have the Spirit of God, I am defeated before I begin."

Yes, even when it takes only one dollar to feed a person, he can starve without that dollar, and that dollar can be as hard for him to get as ten dollars might be for the next person. But when you are in agreement with this teaching of the Master that man shall not live by bread alone, but by every word that proceedeth out of the mouth of God, that it is the Spirit of God that feeds man and clothes him, that the Spirit of God heals, and that Peter and John revealed that the same Spirit that raised up Jesus Christ from the dead will quicken also your mortal body, this Spirit of God will meet your every need. When that Spirit is realized, you will not be concerned with whether the need is for ten dollars or ten hundred dollars because to the Spirit of God there is no limitation in any way or in any form.

With the true idea of gratitude, we have a principle that can result in a change in anyone's life in far less than thirty days if he puts that principle into practice. At every lecture and in every class, or as the result of every lecture and every class, there are some people who come to me or write, telling me that from that moment their lives have been changed. I thank them, but inwardly I smile because I know that it was not the lecture or the class that did it: It was the use they made of it. *It was what they did with what they heard that produced the change.* Should you, for instance, embark upon a program of daily gratitude, not for things, but gratitude for the Spirit of God that underlies this universe, you will find a change in your life that will appear to you as a miracle in thirty days—in less than thirty days.

Be grateful that God is. When you come to that miracle-day in your life—that day when you have the clear realization that God is—you will never again be disturbed by any form of error; you will be able to laugh at it, and that will be the end of it. When that miracle-day arrives and you look out upon the world and witness the horrors it is experiencing, you will begin to understand that when men learn to know that *God is*, these discords will cease. All error will disappear from the face of the earth as we, individually, come to the realization: "God is. What have I to fear? Is there something apart from God? If there were, how could God be infinite? How could God be omnipotent, omnipresent, omniscient—how could God be all in all—if there were reality or power to the discords in life?" So you will find, eventually, that most of the discords in your life touch you because of your acceptance of the universal belief that they have power.

Gratitude for the Presence of God

At any moment you choose, however, you can begin to come into the agreement that if God is, then there is no power in person, place, thing, circumstance, or condition. This is a major principle of The Infinite Way. Then you can say to the man with the withered arm, "Stretch forth thine arm," or to the impotent man, "Rise up and pick up your bed," or to the blind man, "Open your eyes," or to someone else, "What did hinder you? Where is this power that is confining you? What is this power that is holding you back?" As you do that, you will find that there is no such power—you have merely believed in such a power and by your belief in it, have given it the only power it has.

We all must begin to have a real conviction that there is neither good nor evil, that there are not two powers. That does not mean that we shall not often be tempted with sin, disease, death, lack or limitation, accident and all manner of ill, but at each temptation we shall be able to rise up and say, " 'Thou couldest have no power at all against me, except it were given thee from above.'[2] Who said you were a power? I shall not fear what mortal man can do to me. I shall not fear what mortal conditions can do to me." Then we shall find

that, in a very short time, we shall have gained the dominion over this world which was given to us in the beginning.
In the beginning, we were given dominion over the earth
and everything in it, above it, and beneath it, but we have
surrendered that dominion: We gave power to the stars and
astrology; we gave power to the moon; we gave power to the
sun; we gave power to food; we gave power to climate; we
gave power to drugs. Step by step we have surrendered our
dominion.

Now, firm in the conviction that there are not two powers,
we begin to draw back our God-given dominion. It is not
that we, of ourselves, have anything; but *by the grace of God*
we have dominion over all that exists, and therefore, none of
these things has power over us. This requires conscious effort
and continual vigilance. Nobody succeeds on this path by
sitting down and waiting for something to happen; nobody
succeeds by waiting for some unknown God to perform
miracles. Each one of us must be a law unto whatever the
situation is which we are facing. We assume our God-given
dominion by realizing that all power has been invested in
us by the grace of God, and that neither person, place, nor
thing has any power over us. To all men is given the grace
of God. How much of it we keep or how much of it we surrender is what determines our individual experience.

Our gratitude is for the Spirit of God which reveals
Itself as harmony, whether it is harmony in what might be
called some minor, insignificant aspect of life or in a major
and crucial experience. Our gratitude is not a gratitude for
things, but a gratitude for the principle which operates in
every situation. It is a gratitude for the presence of God
in individual affairs. The presence of God may appear as
harmony in human relationships, or harmony of mind, body,

or purse; but actually none of those things could have taken place separate and apart from the demonstration of the presence of God. Millions of people believe that the power to demonstrate God's presence on earth was limited to a period of time two thousand years ago. Many people are worshipping a far-off God that they hope will do something for them on the other side of the grave, but they have long since lost hope that this God can do anything for them here and now. Yet the daily experience of many of our students is a living witness to the fact that God is available. They have proved the availability of God in every situation, circumstance, and condition.

The Proof of Our Gratitude

The proof of our gratitude is, and forever must be, the work that pours out through us. Words or dollars are but symbols of the real gratitude and sometimes most inadequate, though important, symbols. Only the fruitage of the Spirit can bear witness to the true sense of gratitude.

Those who have received some measure of light, illumination, or healing—the benediction of the Christ—through this message, become bearers of the Word unto others, no longer seeking only their own good but seeking more light, ever more light, for the benefit of those who are still in darkness. From this moment on, you should be less interested in what God or The Infinite Way can do for you, and more interested in God's illumining you so that you may be a transparency for this message to the world, that is, to your world, be it wide or narrow in its scope.

To some it may be given to be a light in their homes and in their community; to others to go beyond the environs of their homes or community, carrying this message to the world. It makes no difference in what degree we are called upon to show forth that light. There is no one light more important than another, for without all the others, even the greatest one could not function properly. The great light that we know as Christ Jesus found it necessary that there be disciples. Inasmuch as Jesus Christ left no written word conveying his message to the world, we today would not have his teaching set forth so clearly and concisely, had it not been for those lights lesser than himself, but lights of sufficient magnitude to have left us the word in written form. So remember that the light which is deemed the greatest could not shine in its fulness without the assistance of all the other lights.

You have accepted the truth that God's grace is your sufficiency. Therefore, you are committed not to try to demonstrate things, not to try to demonstrate conditions, not to try to *use* God or *use* Truth; but in all ways to turn within and let Truth use you, let Truth fulfil itself as the harmony of your daily experience. Then, when you are called upon to let that light shine in the experience of those who turn to you, you become a standard-bearer, you become a witness to the power and the presence of God on earth in this age. This is accomplished through your periods of meditation, by opening yourself to the consciousness of God's presence and God's power. It is accomplished by filling yourself with the letter of the Word whether it is the Word as found in our books, *The Letter*, or the recordings—all three—filling yourself as many minutes and as many hours as you can give to it in the day or night, filling yourself with His word, and with the realization of His presence so that you may be the transparency for this light.

It is unthinkable that Jesus would have wasted time praying, meditating, or doing mental work for his health, his supply, his safety, or his security. So must it be with us. As this message permeates our being, we would never dream of using it in connection with our own selves. Having made the contact, It cares for us, It governs us, It sustains, It protects; and therefore, our turning within is for the benefit of those who are still in darkness. In other words, it is as if we were to say, "I know now that there is no use in taking thought for my life, for what I shall eat or what I shall drink or wherewithal I shall be clothed or housed. I have experienced the presence and power of God in my mind and body. I know It is there; I have felt It; now I will let It operate." You will find then that, with no further thought for yourself, the prayer work or the meditation work in which you engage on behalf of those who seek you out or on behalf of the world at large becomes your own treatment, your own prayer, your own fulfilment—a seeking of your own in another's good.

We are the light of the world in proportion as the Spirit of God dwells in us. The mesmerism of "this world" with its newspapers, its radios, and its television would deprive us of our God-given heritage. Attention to these outer things is what deprives us of our contact with God on the inner plane by taking from us the time that is necessary for us to use for our spiritual refreshment, spiritual study, and meditation. Those on this path dare not permit themselves to be ensnared by the pleasures and the sensations of the senses—even by the good things of the senses—to such a degree that they fail to set aside adequate periods for inner contemplation.

Gratitude for Spiritual Teaching

"Seek ye first the kingdom of God."[3] Never forget that passage because it is one of the most important teachings in all Scripture: "Seek ye first the kingdom of God." You can never seek that kingdom until you know what you are seeking, nor can you find it until you know where it is hidden. Give time to pondering the question: "What is the kingdom of God?" The Master revealed quite plainly *where* it is. He never said *what* it is, but he told us where it is—*within you.* So you do not have to go any place to find it. No trips to holy mountains are necessary—no trips to holy temples, no trips anywhere outside of your own inner sanctuary. Go into that inner sanctuary and pray in secret. There, in the silence, you will find it—within yourself. What the experience is after you have found it, the Master did not tell, but he did tell what the fruitage would be—physical health, immortal life, infinite abundance, peace on earth, good will to men. That will be the fruitage of it, but the thing itself, the kingdom of God, is the great gift for which our gratitude should be flowing continually. When an individual finds that kingdom, he never talks about it. There is no language that will describe it, but it can be imparted in meditation without language from teacher to student.

That is the method of our work in The Infinite Way. The meditation on the part of the teacher reveals some of the secrets of this inner kingdom to the consciousness of the student, through silence. It is not done by transmitting messages from one mind to another; the kingdom of heaven cannot be taken by the power of the mind. The things of God are foolishness with man, foolishness to the thinking mind. Who, by taking thought, can learn the spiritual things of life? Nobody. These are not and cannot be transmitted by words. If words could convey the experience, the mystics of the world would long since have put all that they have experienced into books and pamphlets, and we would be reading them and then floating on cloud nine, nineteen, twenty-nine, up to ninety-nine—all ready for number one hundred, and the transition itself.

Spiritual teaching cannot come through the body or through the mind. It can only be transmitted from one Soul to another, and the language of Spirit is silence. Only in the deep, deep silence of an illumined Soul are the secrets transmitted to the Soul of the student who has prepared himself by dedication, not a dedication to the demonstration of things, but to the demonstration of God. When the teacher and the student are so pure in consciousness that neither one is seeking anything for himself, having no desires of an earthly nature, but seeking only to transmit God's grace, then the meditation of a teacher or practitioner results in that receptivity which brings spiritual freedom and spiritual wisdom to the student.

This has always been the way of spiritual teaching. It was the way practiced in the Far East; it was the way in the Near East. It was the way the Master taught his disciples. It was the way Saul of Tarsus received illumination: He did not receive his light sitting with a human teacher of biblical history and Bible lore. It was when he was on the way to Damascus, on the way toward illumination, on the way toward revelation and inspiration, that he met the Christ and the Christ revealed Itself. So with us. When we have left behind earthly desires and earthly longings, when we have left behind a need for the peace that this world giveth and are ready for the peace that the kingdom of God can impart, then are we ready indeed for spiritual illumination.

Too many have been studying for too many years and missing the way because they have believed that spiritual illumination would improve their "things of this world" in some magical way. It does not always do that; in fact, it may temporarily have the opposite effect. Sometimes there comes a period when there is a great deal of deprivation of the things of this world. Saul of Tarsus, you remember, was deprived of his eyesight, blinded, and then, after his illumination, spent nine years in Arabia. The light had not been fully revealed; the fruitage had not appeared in its fulness. So it is often with us. Sometimes it is necessary that we, too, lose our earthly good before our spiritual good reveals itself. Then after that, the lost years of the locusts are restored.

It is not that that necessarily is the price which must be paid. It is only that very often it is the price that is demanded of us because of our inability to turn from the things of this world so that we can devote enough time to the things of "My kingdom." If we voluntarily give the time and the effort necessary to the realization of the spiritual kingdom, we shall gradually evolve into it; but if we so occupy ourselves with the things of the world as to make the things of the Spirit secondary, then sometimes it requires a sharp lesson before we are able to move from the human world into the spiritual.

Do not be too concerned about your own demonstration. Do not feel that financial prosperity is necessarily the sign of your spiritual progress, because there are many wealthy people who have never even heard of spiritual things. Do not think for a moment that physical health is the natural proof of your spirituality, for there are large numbers of physically healthy people who never think of the word God except to use it profanely. Do not try to judge your spiritual development by the condition of your body because physical health is no measure of spirituality. Very often, very, very often, it is when you are in the deepest struggles with your problems that the light of grace breaks through. Sometimes, it is the very severity of those troubles that drives you deep enough so that you come into the awareness of God's grace.

Try not to judge your spiritual progress by whether you have a Cadillac or a Ford, or any car at all. Try not to judge your spiritual progress by whether you happen to be healthy or wealthy today or tomorrow. Remember, the thief on the cross must have been making satisfactory spiritual progress even when he was crucified because that same night he was admitted into paradise. The woman taken in adultery must have been making real spiritual progress for instantly she was forgiven her sins and became a follower of the Master. Never doubt for a moment that if you walk through the valley of the shadow of death and there recognize God's grace, that even then it will not be too late to step out into perfect health. Never feel for a moment that if you are seventy or eighty or ninety that it is too late to attain spiritual illumination for in the moment ye think not, the bridegroom cometh. In that moment, in that twinkling of an eye, all those years drop off your shoulders like pages dropping off a calendar.

Be not too concerned for these daily demonstrations of the world, but never forget that "Whatsoever a man soweth, that shall he also reap."[4] In accord with the measure of spiritual development, ultimately those added things will appear in the form of harmony, because it is your divine right to experience health and abundance. If you do not immediately find yourself in possession of the desired temporal good, physical or financial, if the things of this world are not heaped upon you through your study, do not be too concerned, because that is not the goal of our work. The goal is, "Seek ye first the kingdom of God."[5] Seek Him while He may be found. Seek Him while you are in the mood. Seek the kingdom of God and be assured of this, that despite your day-to-day experience, whether there be harmony today or discord tomorrow, an upset today and a little good the next week—regardless of that, you are on the way if you do not deviate from your basic principle, "I am seeking the kingdom of God, not the kingdom of material demonstration."

• *The True Measure of Gratitude*

This message must be lived. Whatever degree of light it produces in your life will cause those who are ready for it to discern it in you and come to you for some of that which you have. Then you can share pamphlets, books, tape recordings, or monthly *Letters;* you can impart whatever of it you know—*but only to those who seek you out.* You may try to give this teaching to your mother or father, to your child, to your sister or brother, to your husband or wife, or to some other relative; but it will not help them. As much as you would like to take your friends and family into heaven with you, it cannot be done. They cannot accept it until they are ready for it, so it is better to let them come to you, and then you share with them of the light that you have received.

The Infinite Way does not advertise, and yet the word of this message has gone around the world on its own power. In the ten years of The Infinite Way, there has never been an appeal for funds. Nobody has been asked for a contribution. Why? The Spirit of God which gave us this message has financed it, and it has all come through normal and natural ways—voluntary ways.

So it is with you. This message will support you and sustain you, physically, mentally, morally, and financially. You will not have to ask for money; you will not have to plead for it; you will not have to tell anyone that it is his duty to support you. No, the light which you are will do all of that for you and bless all who come into your sphere.

The Infinite Way is a healing message. This message brings healing to all those who are receptive and responsive to it, and since everyone is seeking healing, it must spread in proportion as you are able to be the light, and you are able to be that light in proportion to the amount of time and effort you give to communion. That is the measure of your gratitude.

Across the Desk

The world-wide acceptance and success of The Infinite Way has attracted the attention of some unscrupulous people who are attempting to exploit The Infinite Way or to use my name in order to obtain money fraudulently. Already some of our students have been misled by the false claims of these people. There seems to be no way of preventing these unprincipled people from preying upon the public except as individuals exercise discrimination and prudence. Religion is a prolific field for the unscrupulous because the law usually protects people who operate under its guise. But the law cannot protect you from the machinations of such individuals, nor can The Infinite Way: You either have spiritual discernment or human intelligence to guide you.

Since I myself have never at any time asked you for money, you may be sure that I also have never authorized anyone else to ask you for financial help for themselves or for their activities. Should anyone approach you with a request for funds or with any kind of a proposition to secure your support, monetary or otherwise, on the basis of their alleged association with me or with The Infinite Way, and should you be in doubt as to the proper course of action, you may cable me for information—Inway, Honolulu—and I will gladly and quickly inform you as to whether or not you are dealing with one of our students.

There are people travelling about claiming to be associated with me, or claiming that they are students close to me. Do not accept such claims without some knowledge of their authenticity. It is not difficult to recognize our true students or to learn who they are. Our students use only Infinite Way writings and recordings in their work. They do not beg or borrow. "Silver and gold have I none; but such as I have give I thee,"[6] may be your answer to requests for loans to strangers. "The 'such as I have' I give unto you gladly." There is a legitimate activity of giving, sharing, and helping, but that giving, sharing, and helping must be governed by wisdom. Do not give or lend merely because someone claims to be a patient or a student of The Infinite Way or because someone claims some special association with The Infinite Way or with me. That is flimsy ground for lending or giving.

This admonition is merely a call to exercise wisdom in giving—spiritual wisdom—and is in no sense intended to lessen your giving or sharing since the principles of The Infinite Way are not demonstrated by withholding, miserliness, or a lack of free giving. In fact, true giving is a very important principle of The Infinite Way.

I feel that it is the function of students of The Infinite Way to support its activity. Furthermore, as members of a community it is their responsibility to support the local activities of that community, such as the YMCA, YWCA, Boy Scouts, Girl Scouts, the Community Fund, the Red Cross, and any other worthy activity. Students who are members of fraternal orders should also support the benevolent activities of these orders, and certainly all of us should be liberal in helping to provide educational opportunities and summer camp activities for children. Beyond that, any purely personal appeals for help must be prayerfully considered and accepted or rejected on their merits and not because of claims to some relationship with The Infinite Way.

In the correspondence which comes from every part of the globe and from people at all levels of consciousness, the subject of death, that is, the passing of loved ones from visible sight, is mentioned almost every day. To most of us comes the experience of witnessing the passing of loved ones—parents, aunts, uncles, or grandparents; loved figures of the stage and artistic world who have brought joy and beauty into our lives; and public figures who have for years inspired us by the richness of their lives and by their service to mankind.

In my own experience, I have had almost none of this sadness. My grandparents had left this plane before I knew them; only one aunt and my parents left during my adult years. Otherwise, my life has been strange in that all those with whom I grew up, as well as all the men and women of my twenty-two years in the business world, dropped out of my life when I became a spiritual healer and was listed as a Christian Science practitioner. My world had been a very human world, but it fell away from me as I entered spiritual consciousness. It may be said that I died to my past—to my material life—and was reborn into a spiritual way of life.

For sixteen years, my life was centerd in Christian Science. I do not remember anyone who entered my awareness during those years except Christian Scientists, and only the very active ones at that—readers, practitioners, teachers, lecturers, officers of branch churches and of The Mother Church. These men and women who had consecrated their lives to God were my associates and made up my life-experience for sixteen joyous years. They were wonderful companions on the spiritual way.

When The Infinite Way was born in me, I died again to my past and was reborn in another level of spiritual consciousness. My Christian Science associates dropped away from me as my former business associates had—without a physical dying, just a passing from my visible world. Even my relatives did not die physically, but passed from my view as I ascended in spiritual life. I was born again; and in this new life, I companion with those of The Infinite Way and those on the spiritual path.

Now note this: Into my new life have now appeared some of those associates of my former business life and some of those of my Christian Science life. For me, this answers the great question: Will we meet those who have passed from our sight?

Yes, we shall meet those of our own household—those who grow with us and catch up to us, or those who have gone ahead and with whom we catch up. Those intended to be our eternal companions are never lost to our spiritual awareness. Even if there is an interval of separation, we catch up to them or they catch up to us.

To saint as well as to sinner, there comes a time of separation from the past. This may come as it does to many of us in what the world terms death, or it may come as it has to me, by a spiritual progression out of past lives but without a dying out of them. Whichever way it comes, the important thing to remember is this: When you die out of "this world," you will leave all your material possessions at the probate court which is always waiting at the exit to collect your belongings! *The only property you can take with you is the degree of enlightened consciousness which you attain here.* No one can strip you of that illumined consciousness, so spend your time here endeavoring to attain all the illumination you can.

If you die to your past through spiritual progression, you will have but few material possessions beyond those necessary to your immediate needs because you will have dedicated your earnings to spiritual purposes. Even though you will always be abundantly supplied while on the path of spiritual illumination, you will not burden yourself with too many temporal cares along the way.

Lay up for yourselves rich treasures—spiritual treasures of the Soul. Bring to each "death," whichever way it takes place, not too much baggage to shed, but rich treasures of illumination, dedication, and ordination. Each of us prospers spiritually in proportion to his devotion to God and the word of God.

The wise virgins were those who kept oil in their own lamps. Wise students of The Infinite Way are not concerned with whether their friends or relatives are going along the path with them: They are prepared to leave father, mother, sister, brother, husband, wife, friends, and business associates and to go on alone with God. We keep ourselves filled with spiritual truth; we meditate; we companion with those on our path; we unfold according to a divine plan, and when friends pass from our sight we recognize that they are but attaining another level of consciousness. When we reach a plateau from which we take off for higher and deeper spiritual experiences, we leave our old world with no regrets, but rather with eagerness to view the grand horizon.

This is the season of Thanksgiving. An entire day devoted to the giving of thanks provides students of The Infinite Way with an unusual opportunity to look behind the visible scene and witness the many special reasons for thanksgiving this year. Even though we, as aspirants on the spiritual path, have learned the true nature of gratitude and have learned to be grateful every day in the year, nevertheless, it must be apparent to all of us that it is only through the grace of God that men in a materialistic era have set aside one special day of the year to be dedicated wholly to thanksgiving. I joy in that.

In reviewing the year, I note that it has been brought to human attention, and recognized and acknowledged on a wider scale than ever before, that material or physical force will not solve international problems. Treaties and promises continue to be broken to such an extent that few people and even few nations trust the word of another, or even their own word except when it suits the purpose of the moment. Strange as it may seem, that in itself is good reason for thanksgiving because from it we shall learn to "cease … from man, whose breath is in his nostrils."[7] Eventually, all will be compelled to place *complete* reliance on the Invisible which is truly the Infinite Omnipotent, omnipresent. When faith reaches that point, the world will be saved.

Throughout the world, there is evidence of man's inhumanity to man—intolerance, prejudice, and bigotry. That, too, is cause for thanksgiving because a growing spiritual awareness is evident as these particular evils are exposed to the world instead of being covered up, hidden, and secretly practiced. Now we must pray with a greater depth of understanding that the eyes of the blind be opened and the ears of the deaf be unstopped so that the vision of the great Master may be revealed: "And call no man your father upon the earth: for one is your Father, which is in heaven."[8]

In The Infinite Way we have a truly great reason for thanksgiving: We have learned and demonstrated that we need not reform people, or change them humanly, but rather our work is to destroy *material sense* and thus *free mankind from its only bondage*. We have discovered the secret of the destruction of material sense, and my special reason for giving thanks is that some students are uniting with me around the globe and around the clock to realize, with signs following, that material sense is but "the arm of flesh." At present, this group has the secret which all our students soon will understand and prove.

Above all, I can have no greater reason for thanksgiving than to know that Infinite Way students will give a day to spiritual communion, prayer, and thanksgiving and will dedicate this day every year to the lessening of material sense through the realization of grace.

❖ 12 ❖

Tithing with Melchizedek

THE SCRIPTURAL RECORD of the birth of Christ Jesus is the account of a little child, born to a very insignificant couple with no status in the world, a Jewish carpenter and his wife, who are on their way to Jerusalem to bring tithes for the annual celebration at the temple. If you read this story with the eyes of the world, you will miss its real importance. Here are two obscure and unknown people to whom a child is born, and yet instantly something unusual takes place: Wise men come to pay homage to that child, and they come bringing their choicest gifts. From every direction, people come, all of them bringing gifts in recognition of That to which they are paying homage. Neither Mary nor Joseph made any effort to attract such attention to themselves, and certainly the baby could do nothing but lie there, perhaps crying a little and sleeping a great deal more. Yet, without a single effort, people came from near and far to bring their offerings, their worship, and their adoration.

No infant of itself is of such importance as to attract that amount of attention. Usually only parents, grandparents, brothers, or sisters are drawn to an infant. Then what was it that drew unto this particular baby the wise men and worshippers from great distances except that which this babe represented? Something was present in this child and that Something was the Christ. It was not the child, itself, which brought such adoration to it, but the Christ of which this child was the embodiment.

There is a Presence and a Power which human beings can never explain and which human beings can never see. Only wise men, those of an illumined state of consciousness, can perceive spiritual entity embodied in a little child. Only those gifted with spiritual wisdom could know or be drawn to that spiritual light.

> When Herod the king had heard these things, he was troubled. ... And when he had gathered all the chief priests and scribes of the people together, he demanded of them where Christ should be born. ...
>
> And he sent them to Bethlehem, and said, Go and search diligently for the young child. ...
>
> And ... behold, the angel of the Lord appeareth to Joseph in a dream, saying, Arise, and take the young child and his mother, and flee into Egypt ... for Herod will seek the young child to destroy him.[1]

When those in high authority heard about the young child, they were afraid. Had they understood the nature of the Christ, they would never have feared because they would have known that the Christ is not a temporal power. The Christ never aspires to place or position. The Christ is always of a constructive nature. No one need ever fear the Christ, and yet wherever the Christ appears, those in authority tremble and fear and try to do away with It.

Christhood Is a Recognition of Divine Sonship

The Christ is not a man or a woman. The Christ is a divine state of consciousness which appears on earth *as* a man or a woman. It is not limited to one man or one woman but appears in some degree as every man and every woman on earth. There is no one—no one so lowly—who has not entertained some measure of the Christ. This is true of everyone. Christhood is the fulness of that transcendental quality and character which recognizes the infinite, divine nature of individual being. Those who, like the Master, attain It in its fulness are the Messiahs, Saviors, or spiritual revelators of the world.

Saviors have appeared on earth from time to time; and always what have they come to earth to reveal? Their message is that Christhood is a spiritual entity and identity which is the reality of every individual in the world. That which makes them Messiahs or revelators is their perception of Christhood, not only as the reality of their own being, but as the reality of individual you and me. Only in the degree in which they perceive the universal nature of Christhood, are they the full embodiment of the Christ. There would be no evidence of Christhood in them, if they told only of their own Christhood, because the very telling of it would be proof that Christhood had not been realized. Christhood can be recognized in that individual who comes to earth to reveal *your* Christhood and to enable you and me to bring forth more of the light than we are showing forth at any moment.

Any quality of good that we are bringing through into expression is a measure of Christhood since we, of ourselves, have no such qualities. The mere fact that within us is the capacity to be just, wise, benevolent, forgiving, loving, or cooperative indicates that Christhood is within us and that It can be brought into expression in greater measure than any of us has yet attained or even believed possible That is the function of the Savior. The Savior is not a man: The Savior is that state of consciousness which appeared at the birth of Jesus Christ, as It has at other times, and which has been recognized by all those of spiritual vision or intuition—by the wise men of all ages. The wise men recognized that state of consciousness in the child of Bethlehem, a consciousness which, in its full development, enabled Christ Jesus to say in substance, "That which I am showing forth is the Father within me, so you can go and do likewise because It is your Father as well as my Father."

> And when they were come into the house, they saw the young child with Mary his mother, and fell down, and worshipped him: and when they had opened their treasures, they presented unto him gifts; gold, and frankincense, and myrrh. ...[2]
>
> And suddenly there was with the angel a multitude of the heavenly host praising God, and saying, Glory to God in the highest, and on earth peace, good will toward men.[3]

The wise men brought gifts; the birds sang; the angels hovered about; the stars danced in the skies; and all manner of spiritual phenomena took place at this birth of the Christ. So it ever has been and so it always will be at the moment of the Christ's appearing as your individual consciousness. At the moment that you transcend your human sense of "I" and realize the nature of the Christ as your being, thereby relaxing your personal efforts, wise men will come to you bringing gifts, songs will be sung, and praise will be uttered.

The wise bring their gifts to the Christ. One who is imbued with the Christ does not have to go out and earn these gifts or do something to get them, or even deserve them. The wise unite in offering their wealth, their homage, and their adoration to that Christ-hood. It would make no difference to the wise whether the Christ appeared as an insignificant child born to a lowly couple or whether It appeared as the son of Caesar Augustus. The wise will offer themselves wherever and whenever Christhood appears.

Christhood, spiritual illumination, comes as the grace of God. No one can receive It by his own efforts or by his own labor, yet, paradoxically, no one can receive It without effort and without labor. Either in our past or present experience—somewhere in the on-goingness of life, grace touches each Soul. Then for some reason unknown to human beings, that individual who has been brutish, that individual who has been dictatorial, that individual who has been evil begins to have his thoughts turned to good and probably in some one life passes out of that particular experience a much finer individual than he was when he came in through the experience of birth. Then you may know that such an individual has been touched by divine grace, and his ascent has begun.

This is true individually and collectively. Society is in no way perfect either humanly or spiritually, but the wise measure progress and development over a long period of time rather than in terms of the achievements of any single segment of time For example, there is little evidence of spiritual evolution in the throwing of an atomic bomb, but the seeds of a developing spiritual consciousness in the citizens of the nation throwing the bomb are apparent in the amount of horror expressed by those citizens when they learn of the use of the bomb. When it is known that the nation as a whole is not and never was in favor of such action, even for the purpose of self-preservation, then it would seem that spiritual Presence and Power are becoming more evident in human consciousness. Furthermore, there are signs of a growing spiritual awareness throughout the world in the conviction that slavery is neither right nor moral. Spiritually, the world today is on a higher level than during any previous age. This evolutionary process is evident in an increasing number of individuals and is appearing on earth collectively as a better society.

The Nature of the Christ

Scripture tells us that we must become as little children, taking no thought for tomorrow, but living always in the realization of *nowness*. The nature of the Christ is symbolized by the guilelessness, trust, and faith of a little child. A child has less of the sense of "I" to overcome; he knows nothing of having to battle the world for a livelihood; he is under no impulsion to protect himself from evil people—he knows little or nothing of the world's beliefs. The child knows that everything is all right, but probably is unaware of the fact that everything is all right because of the loving care of mother or father. With him there is just the joy of pure being. As we approach that childlike state of consciousness, we realize that it is not any conscious effort of our own that brings the world to us with its offerings—the wise men bringing gifts—but rather it is this inherent entity or identity, this innate spiritual nature, which is forever drawing unto itself its own.

Within each of us, there is that which is forever drawing unto itself its own. We may call that the Father within; we may call it the Father-Mother God; or we may call it the Christ. Whatever it is, it is of a nature, character, and purpose which draws unto itself its own; and it can do that best as we relax from personal struggle and effort—relinquish the sense of I-ness. This relaxing in the Spirit will not come without personal effort; only now that personal effort is not aimed at drawing good to us, but at drawing out into expression that good which is already within us. Heretofore, effort, for the most part, has been directed toward earning a living or gaining fame and fortune—always toward getting—whereas effort rightly directed is toward the realization of the Christ, the Infinite Invisible. Therein lies the effort.

This principle applies to the solving of a problem whether for ourselves or for another. The solution of a problem is accomplished in proportion to the amount of effort we can bring to *relaxing from effort*. In other words, it is very much like waiting out a storm instead of going into it head on. It is a constant remembrance that "this too shall pass," and then sitting quietly, or moving about carrying on one's affairs in the realization that whatever the name or nature of the "this," it will pass, not by any concerted efforts of our own, directed toward the achievement of some specific purpose, nor by human will or supernatural powers, but by virtue of the nothingness of this "it" which we have been honoring by fighting.

"The battle is not yours, but God's … stand ye still, and see the salvation of the Lord."[4] This can only be described as the effort of effortlessness, the effort which is necessary to be quiet in the face of a storm or in the face of the discords of human experience so that these, too, may pass. These discords will not pass while we are fighting them, because the very act of fighting them makes of them a reality, perpetuating them in our consciousness. The discord or the problem has no externalized existence; it exists only as a mental image in our own thought, and as we retire to this inner sanctuary and wait, the storm passes. Afterwards, we learn that there never was a storm outside of us; the storm was within our own being. Outside, all was peaceful and serene. The very fact that our neighbors down the street have been unaware of this storm that we have been battling is evidence that it existed in us. It did not exist for them because they were not inside of us. That is the only place the storm, the sin, the disease, the lack or limitation has existence—*within us*. If we can become still enough, quiet enough, and if we can acquire some of David's assurance of God's grace, then this will also pass. Christhood is the recognition of this truth. The degree of our Christhood can be measured by the degree of quiet and peace that we can find while waiting for "this" to pass.

John Burroughs gave us the entire secret of Christhood in his poem, "Waiting." He must have known that what he was saying was not true of human beings because too many human beings have been waiting for too long without finding "their own." He must have known that it was the spirit of tranquility and peace which he attained within himself that made it possible for him to write, "My own shall come to me."

When people say, "Oh, I just trust God to do it," very often it is not done for them, because human beings, as such, have no God to do it for them. That which they call God and which they are expecting to perform some desired thing for them has no existence except as a mental concept within them. They wait for a non-existent God to bring about some specific good and they wait in vain. But the finding of peace within, through the realization of our inner divine Selfhood, is the attainment of that which draws unto Itself everything necessary for Its unfoldment and development.

In the tranquility of the Soul, spiritual awareness develops. Spiritual awareness is the realization of the nothingness of storms or problems. It is a state of consciousness which knows that the creative Principle of this universe is also the maintaining and sustaining influence of the universe. We say, and sometimes very glibly, "Spiritual consciousness heals," or "Spiritual consciousness is a redeeming power," but what is spiritual consciousness? If, in meditation, you ask yourself, "What is spiritual consciousness?" the answer will come:

Spiritual consciousness is your awareness that I am, that I exist, that My presence at the center of your being lives your life for you. Spiritual consciousness is your awareness of the nothingness of the thoughts and things of this world. It is an awareness of My peace at the center of your being—your awareness that My grace is your sufficiency. The very moment that you attain the first glimpse of God's grace as your sufficiency in all things, you have attained a measure of spiritual consciousness.

The more that spiritual consciousness develops and evolves in you, the more assurance you achieve of God's grace. Then there is less personal effort in living this human life; less effort and personal strength are needed to surmount the problems of life. The day comes when not only are there no problems of life, but when that day finally does arrive, and the world comes to us bearing its gifts and showering its glories upon us, we find ourselves saying, "I don't deserve this." That is true because these gifts are not brought to you or to me any more than gifts are brought to the person of some reigning monarch: The gifts are not brought to the person but to the office of which the monarch is the symbol.

The world's peace, grace, and good are not brought and laid at our feet because of you or of me. No, they are brought because of Christhood, because of the tranquility that has come through the realization of a divine Presence and a divine Power at the heart and the center, not only of our own being, but at the heart and center of all individual being. Christhood is Christhood only in proportion as it recognizes Christhood as a universal state of being. When it sets itself up as Christhood to the exclusion of all others, it is not Christhood. Christhood is the recognition of God as the central theme of man's being. The very moment that you realize God to be the activity of every human being, every animal, vegetable, and mineral, you are showing forth

Christhood, but in order to show It forth, it is necessary to recognize Its universality. Do you see what happens to your enemy in your recognition of the universality of Christhood? The enemy disappears. Do you see what happens to the neighbor you love as yourself? Even that neighbor disappears. There are no longer friends, and there are no longer enemies. Friends and enemies merge into the one Self, and that Self is the God-Self appearing as infinite individuality—as an infinity of people and things.

Paying Homage to the Christ

Every one of us must acknowledge the spiritual identity of each other, and that acknowledgment is our tithe to Melchizedek, just as the wise men's recognition of the Christ in Jesus led them to Bethlehem with their gifts. Even Abraham who was the father of the Hebrews which places him in somewhat the same relationship to them as the relationship of Jesus to the Christians—even Abraham paid tithes to Melchizedek. It makes no difference who you are or what your name or station in life, as a human being, you must always pay tithes, always lay your all at the feet of that which was never born and will never die. Melchizedek was never born and has never died because Melchizedek is the Spirit of God appearing as individual being, that is, appearing as you and as me. It is that Spirit of God to which every human being must bow, must bend his knee, must tithe, must share, must give, must acknowledge in one way or another. The tithe of Abraham to Melchizedek is exactly the same act as was that of the wise men in bringing gifts to the Babe of Bethlehem. It was their recognition of spiritual identity and of Christhood.

Every time that you give inner recognition to Christhood anywhere on earth, you are bringing your gifts to the Babe; you are tithing with Melchizedek. You are recognizing that no matter how great or noble you are in your humanhood, you are still less, far less, than your spiritual Selfhood or the spiritual Selfhood of others. Jesus bore witness to this in denying himself, when he said, "I can of mine own self do nothing ...[5] My doctrine is not mine, but his that sent me."[6] That was his tithing and his form of bringing gifts to the spiritual identity of individual being. No one should miss the experience of laying his gifts at the feet of the Christ, of tithing with Melchizedek. Not one of us can or should want to escape the experience of bending the knee to the Christhood of each other.

As we recognize the Christhood of each other, we rest in a calm assurance that no one will harm us by any destructive or dishonest act and, in that resting, we meet all those who cross our path with tranquility and with the absolute conviction that we are safe and in good company. This will be true even when we meet with our particular Goliath because we shall know that with all his seeming strength, a little pebble—one tiny little word—will be enough: "I am; thou art. We are one in Christ. The Spirit of God is your life, your soul, your being." That simple realization is our pebble. That is the only stone we need against any Goliath—just the words, "I am; thou art. We are one."

The Master told Peter that only the Father within, spiritual consciousness, enabled Peter to recognize Jesus as the Christ. So it is that only spiritual consciousness in you will enable you to perceive the Christ in your neighbor. It is not enough to make an affirmation or statement of truth to the effect that Christ is the center of all being or that every man is a child of God. That may be enough to make a person begin thinking, but it is not enough to reach the goal of Christhood. There must eventually come an actual state of consciousness within you in which you, yourself, perceive Christhood as man's real being.

Never be satisfied with a statement of truth, regardless of how true it may be or how noble or divine the individual may be who said it. The mere fact that you have read or have heard some statement of truth which Jesus made will not make your demonstration. There must come to our hearts an actual conviction. To our Soul must come an actual awakening to these truths before they can be made evident in our experience. The Master warned us that not all who cry, "Christ, Christ," will enter in. Not all who make affirmations of truth, regardless of how truthful those affirmations may be, will enter spiritual consciousness, because spiritual consciousness is only attained as it becomes a state of conviction in the region of the heart, not up in the realm of the head. It may well be that our first glimpse of truth enters our consciousness through the mind. We take it in through our intellect, but that truth has not yet become the Christhood of our being. However, when that same recognition that Abraham had for Melchizedek or that the Wise Men had for Jesus comes to our Soul, when we perceive within our own being, "Yes, thou art the Christ. Christ is the truth of being. Christ is the real nature of every individual. Christ is that center of my being which draws unto itself its own"—then, in that moment of recognition, is the transition made. There is for each one of us a point, a time, or a place of transition when these intellectually known truths become spiritually discerned consciousness.

To attain this spiritual discernment, it is necessary that we abide in stillness at the center of our being and loose these judgments of the world or judgments of each other, resting back and letting the storm pass, letting go of the arguments of material sense, letting the material estimates of God, man, and the universe drop away from us without fighting them or battling them or trying to change them.

The degree of our struggle is only the degree in which our humanhood opposes our spiritual nature, but for some that struggle is intense. There is a great deal of humanhood to be overcome, and the difficult thing to understand is that it is not only evil humanhood which must be overcome, but good as well. Good human beings oftentimes have a hard struggle to overcome their sense of good humanhood, because it is pleasant and satisfying to cling to one's goodness. On the other hand, those who are aware of certain undesirable qualities know that they should make an effort to get rid of them. The good people, however, believe that their human qualities are so good that they like to keep them. Christhood comes to our individual consciousness as we see less and less of the need to struggle in the world. The less we engage in a battle with "this world," the more of Christhood that is unfolding.

In Scripture, we see Abraham tithing with Melchizedek; we see the Wise Men bringing their gifts to the Babe; we see Peter recognizing the Christhood of Jesus. So also we watch a great symbology in pilgrimages to temples or holy places. It makes no difference what form of symbology is used as long as there is an act of recognition. What that act is, is unimportant, but to each one must come an occasion for using some form of symbology. What that form is, must come as a dictate of the heart, not as a ceremony demanded by some rule or regulation.

In other words, when, as an expression of the state of his own consciousness, a person places a flower on an altar, lights a candle or a piece of incense, removes his hat, tips it, or places it on his head, or takes off his shoes, it is his recognition of that which he acknowledges as Christhood. Until there is that recognition, Christ has not yet come to the heart.

Until the moment comes when this tithe or gift to the Babe is given as a conscious act and until such time as the heart dictates and compels one to perform an act of purification or an act of sacrifice or an act of devotion, the Christ has not yet come to individual awareness, and the letter of truth is dead and it killeth. The letter of truth is of no avail until the heart has yielded, until the Soul has paid homage to the Christ somewhere, somehow, in some one, or in some thing. To each one it comes in a different way; to each one it comes in a different form. To each one the recognition and the symbology may appear in an original and distinctive way, but at some time in every individual's experience, the Christ is born, and that birth is recognized by an act of devotion. Let us not forget this: The birth of the Christ is recognized by a voluntary act of devotion. Until that act of devotion has come, the Christ is still the expected Messiah, and we are either awaiting the Messiah or we are waiting for the second coming of the Messiah; but we have not yet attained the Christ in our heart. When however, there is a voluntary and spontaneous act of homage, an act of sacrifice, an act of love taking place within our being, we may know that the Christ is born in us.

THE CHRIST[7]

The Christ or Son of God is a Spirit. We, as human beings, are as the branch that is cut off and withereth, that barren state of consciousness described by the Master in the fifteenth chapter of John. At some moment in our experience, by the grace of God, and only by the grace of God, the realization of this dawns in consciousness; and thus is the Christ conceived in us.

Since this experience usually takes place as a direct result of longing, seeking, and striving after God, it may be said to be conceived of a virgin. Indeed, it can only be conceived in that purity of consciousness which seeks illumination and which is engaged in constant, conscious devotion to God.

As the idea of the Christ grows in us, it displaces misconceptions of life heretofore entertained and often brings with it a period of distress and discord as the finite sense begins to yield to the new Influence. The limited sense of self is painfully yielding to the realization of eternal and immortal Selfhood. Then, one day, in the midst of devotion to God and while paying tribute in love and in a surrender of the personal self, the Christ is born in us.

The deep humility, which accompanies the realization of the nothingness and barrenness of the self, is like unto the manger of old, since there is no room now for the trappings and elegancies of self. Self has been stripped bare. Now quickly, the Christ announces Itself, permeating every facet of our being with Its light. All our senses are alert to the new Presence we are entertaining. Recognizing Its nature, that which corresponds to the Wise Men in us—our intelligence, our love, our devotion—pays homage to That which is now recognized as Savior, redeemer, healer, the very presence of Love, Itself.

Human sense, in ourselves and in the world, is ever in opposition to That which eventually dissolves all that is human and finite, and for this reason we entertain our Babe in secrecy and in silence—in the inner, hidden Egypt of consciousness.

As spiritual unfoldment continues, and we become more and more assured of the Light and more conscious of Its function as That which heals, redeems, saves, inspires, and illumines; we find ourselves strengthened in faith and understanding. Inner communion deepens, and the miracles begin to be evident to those about us.

Our new-found strength of character is quickly noticed: the shining face sometimes appearing even as a halo above one's head; the firmness in authority and decisiveness in approach becoming increasingly apparent. The dull waters of the human mind now turn to the wine of inspiration as the wedding, or union, of God and man is witnessed and celebrated. Sickness gives place to health; doubt, fear, and sin disappear at the very approach of the Christ; and even dead humanity comes to life as eternal Life reveals Its shining Light.

In Its presence, there is no lack, since It, Itself, fills every part of consciousness. It becomes our food and drink as well as our inspiration and wisdom. No longer do we seek the things and thoughts of the world, since now there is a continuous flow within of streams of living waters. The staff of life is ever at hand; the meat of divine wisdom becomes our strength of mind and body; and no more need we "live by bread alone."

In the earliest experience of the Christ, the discords and inharmonies of sense are healed and removed: the defects of character; the ills of the flesh; the mental and moral sicknesses; the bondage to lack and limitation. Through the unfolding revelation of the gospel, ignorance yields to the light of spiritual wisdom. Material and mental might and power are now replaced with divine grace. The "arm of flesh" is supplanted by "the spirit of the Lord."

Later, much later, comes the crucifixion—the destruction of even the harmony and good of human experience. Through the crucifixion of good personal selfhood, comes the ascension, as the fulness of the Christ—the body and being of the Christ-Self—is revealed within us. Our humanhood, in its evil and sickly sense, has long since disappeared. Even the good of human experience gives way to the realization of Christhood. No longer is there good or evil, but only the glory that was with us since before the world began—Christhood.

CHRIST HEALING[8]

The Christ ministry is a healing ministry. When John, the Baptist, asked if Jesus were in truth the Christ, the Master had only one answer:

> Go and show John again those things which ye do hear and see: The blind receive their sight, and the lame walk, the lepers are cleansed, and the deaf hear, the dead are raised up, and the poor have the gospel preached to them.[9]

No word written or spoken about the Christ would be complete without calling attention to Its function as healer, supplier, and redeemer.

To heal through Christ-consciousness, it is necessary to transcend thought. Even though a meditation begins as a contemplation of Truth, it must rise into the higher realm of silent awareness before the healing can be accomplished. To begin a healing meditation, we become a state of receptivity, listening for what may be revealed from within.

Often a passage of truth comes into thought, repeating itself over and over, such as, "henceforth know we no man after the flesh."[10] After this has repeated itself several times, or after we have consciously repeated it, thought slows down as we ponder the meaning of the statement, "henceforth know we no man after the flesh." Now we perceive that man is not flesh, but consciousness—spiritual being, spiritual qualities. We discern that not only is there a creative Principle which produces Its own image and likeness, but that It is the sustaining Principle of life. Its creation must necessarily be of Its own essence—Life, Love, Spirit, Soul—and this is the nature of man. It is seen that the visible man, whether sick or well, is not that man; but that the Christ or spiritual Self is truly man. This man is not subject to the law of the flesh—not even harmonious flesh—but is subject only to Christ, divine sonship.

It is not long before we reach the end of such mental cogitation or contemplation and settle into a quiet, peaceful state of receptivity into which no though intrudes. In this state of receptivity, the healing Christ or Spirit of God takes over, maintaining a tranquility and peace, a spiritual "peace, be still," and from this emanates a healing grace which envelops us or our patient; and through this healing grace, harmony becomes apparent and tangible in our experience.

THE MASTER SPEAKS[11]
A Review by Richard Witwell[12]

If I truly understand Joel, I am sure that I can say there is not a vestige of egotism in what he writes, but rather a very deep and profound humility. And it is from that *ground* that all that is lovely in his teaching has its origin. It gives me personally the deepest joy to realize that this is so, even as in our beloved brother H. T. H. whom we all love. It implies a great and deep and liberating selflessness. And this is the ground, as it is also the authentic sign of all true *mysticism*, wherever it is found. And mysticism, rightly understood, is the one true language that has been spoken from the beginning, and through which Christ, our ageless Christ, reveals-Christ, our Savior and Redeemer even from the beginning. It is the language of the Spirit, expressing a mutual and common understanding, wherever it is spoken. And those in whom this consciousness awakens have an intuitive realization of instant fellowship. And "their conversation (that is, their mutual intercourse) is in heaven," for spiritually are they treading on heavenly ground, and heaven is flowing between.

It is from this consciousness that dear Joel is writing, and expressing his vision of truth, his spiritual realization, coming to him so beholdingly and exultantly. What I have said implies that the words and teaching pouring from his pen are not unequal but are flowing in a pure stream from the highlands of that realization. His words are his own, and yet they are not his own. Their origin is in the selflessness of Christ—the Divine humility, so amazing and so wonderful, the very fountain source of all that is real and true and lovely in our human life. Apart from that there is only defacement.

How wonderful the revealing that is taking place today, here and there and everywhere, and the unfolding of the knowledge of God that is to save the world from an otherwise impending absolute calamity! As yet it is manifest but in the twos and threes, to whom the enlightenment has come. They have sought and found that upper Room, where is the Presence, and where God's *kingdom* is revealed in a heavenly and perfect fellowship one with another.

The book covers a wide ground, but it is all of a piece; and the message is one, springing from its lovely heavenly source and power-station—in the realization that God only is our life, our true life forever and ever. The kingdom of heaven in man's experience is the expansion of this realization.

ACROSS THE DESK

As I sit at my desk on Halekou Place, with wide-open windows, a gentle breeze blowing through the house, bright sunshine, and outside in the garden many kinds and colors of tropical flowers, it is difficult to realize that I am writing about Christmas. However, in my mind, Christmas has nothing to do with snow scenes, a red-coated, heavily furred Santa, nor with lighted Christmas trees a-glitter with tinsel and colored balls. Christmas was born in a setting more nearly like the atmosphere of Hawaii with its palm trees, sunny hills and valleys—the Asian gentleness and Roman harshness mixed together in a great melting pot.

Thought travels back to the Inn on that momentous occasion. Some call it the birth of Jesus; others see in it the revelation of the Christ. I see it as the introduction into human consciousness of that which is to save the world from self-destruction. I see the vision of the messenger stating the law in "ye have heard it said of old," and now declaring, "but I say unto you," and thereby showing forth the new dispensation—the life of grace. Christmas ushers in to the receptive human consciousness the new day, the new dimension, a life by grace instead of a life under the law, a life which does not violate the law, but which transcends it.

In the world, ye shall have the law with its rewards and punishments. In grace, ye shall know only freedom and peace. In the world, one power will ever overcome, destroy, or remove another power. Under grace, there are no powers—only joy and rejoicing. Christmas ushers into human experience the awareness of God, and therefore ye need not fight: God's grace is your sufficiency. "Put up thy sword."[13] Christmas is a revelation: Harmony is achieved "not by might, nor by power, but by my spirit."[14] The Christmas message is, "Resist not evil."[15] Resistance is the weapon of this world. "Put up thy sword," physical and mental, and see the saving power of grace.

Christmas calls us from law to grace. Christmas reveals harmony through love instead of fear. Christmas teaches that health and holiness are achieved without physical or mental laws, but through pure grace. Christmas is the message of peace on earth revealed by Christ Jesus, the messenger, who proved the truth of his message without carnal weapons, physical might, or mental control in his life by grace—and he told us to go and do likewise.

To make Christmas live for you, accept the messenger and his message: "Put up thy sword"—rise above physical and mental powers and rest in His grace. "My peace I give unto you: not as the world [and its weapons] giveth"[16] but my peace—God's grace.

SCRIPTURAL REFERENCES AND NOTES

THE INFINITE WAY LETTERS 1957

1. JANUARY: OUT OF DARKNESS-LIGHT

1. Delivered at Caxton Hall, London, April, 1956.
2. Wherever "I" appears in italics, the reference is to God.
3. Matthew 5:14–16
4. Reprinted by permission from *The Seeker*, Perth, Western Australia, September, 1956.
5. Acts 9:11
6. Mark 4:25
7. Sheldon Cheney. *Men Who Have Walked with God* (New York: Alfred A. Knopf, 1945).

2. FEBRUARY: MAJOR PRINCIPLES OF THE INFINITE WAY

1. An article written by the author for *The Seeker*, September, 1956, and reprinted by permission from *The Seeker*, Perth, Western Australia.
2. Matthew 6: 25
3. Luke 12: 32
4. Psalm 23:1
5. Matthew 11: 3–5
6. Exodus 3:5
7. Psalm 139:8
8. Psalm 23:4
9. Isaiah 26:3
10. Exodus 33:14
11. John 8:32
12. Luke 15:31
13. John 10:30
14. Mark 4:25
15. John 19:11
16. John 5:8
17. John 14:27
18. John 4:32
19. John 4:10
20. Hebrews 13:5
21. Matthew 28:20
22. Psalm 46:6
23. Isaiah 41:13, 17, 18
24. II Corinthians 3:17

3. March: Understanding the Body

1. John 10:30
2. I Corinthians 6:19
3. I Timothy 3:16
4. John 10:30
5. John 12:45
6. John 16:28
7. Matthew 23:9
8. I Corinthians 15:50
9. Romans 3:20
10. Jeremiah 12:12
11. Job 34:15
12. Zechariah 14:12
13. Romans 8:13
14. Isaiah 40:6, 7
15. John 6:63
16. Job 19:26
17. Joel 2:28
18. Isaiah 4:5
19. Luke 3:6
20. Psalm 145:4
21. John 1:4
22. Job 19:26
23. Joel 2:28
24. I Corinthians 15:50
25. Romans 3:20
26. Jeremiah 12:12
27. Romans 12:2
28. Matthew 3:17
29. John 1:4
30. Job 19:26
31. Romans 8:13
32. Galatians 6:8
33. Matthew 4:4
34. Matthew 6:19, 20
35. John 6:35
36. John 7:32
37. John 14:1
38. John 12:24
39. II Corinthians 5:1
40. II Corinthians 5:4
41. Galatians 5:6
42. John 16:7

4. April: Resurrection

1. John 2:19
2. Ibid
3. Hebrews 13:5
4. Matthew 28:20
5. Isaiah 30:21
6. Isaiah 60:1
7. Luke 2:14
8. Matthew 26:52
9. Luke 23:34
10. Psalm 46:6
11. John 10:30
12. Isaiah 26:3
13. John 15:4

5. MAY: THE CHRIST, THE PRESENCE IN YOU

1. Matthew 6:1–5
2. Joel S. Goldsmith. *The Infinite Way* (San Gabriel, California, Willing Publishing Company, 1956).
3. Romans 7:19
4. Galatians 2:20
5. I John 4:4
6. 1 John 5:30
7. Isaiah 45:22
8. Isaiah 44:8
9. 1 Galatians 2:20
10. Revelations 12:10
11. 1 Joel S. Goldsmith. *The Art of Meditation.* (New York: Harper & Brothers, 1956).

6. JUNE: THE SECRET OF THE HEALING PRINCIPLE

1. Joel S. Goldsmith. *Practicing the Presence.* (London: L. N. Fowler & Co. Ltd., 1956).

7. JULY: SUPPLY

1. Isaiah 2:8
2. Joel S. Goldsmith. *The Art of Meditation* (New York: Harper & Brothers, 1956).
3. Isaiah 2:22
4. Matthew 6:19
5. John 5:30
6. John 14:10
7. I Samuel 3:9
8. John 14:27
9. Hebrews 13:5
10. Ruthi:16
11. For a further explanation, see "To Him That Hath," Joel S. Goldsmith. *Practicing the Presence* (London: L. N. Fowler & Co. Ltd., 1956).
12. Luke 15:31
13. Reprinted by permission from the *Science of Thought Review*, Chichester, England. June, 1957.

8. AUGUST: YOUR NAMES ARE WRITTEN IN HEAVEN

1. Psalm 118:6
2. II Chronicles 20:17
3. Joel S. Goldsmith. *The Infinite Way* (San Gabriel, California: Willing Publishing Company, 1956).
4. By the author. Reprinted by permission from *The Seeker*, Perth, Western Australia, June, 1957.

9. SEPTEMBER: THE PRAYER OF MYSTICISM

1. Matthew 6:9
2. Psalm23:1
3. Luke 12:22, 30–32
4. John 10:30
5. Exodus 3:5
6. John 16:15
7. John 14:11
8. II Corinthians 12:9
9. *Ibid.*
10. *Ibid.*
11. I Corinthians 2:9
12. John 4:32
13. Psalms 37:3
14. John 7:37
15. John 14:27
16. Zechariah 4:6
17. Mark 4:25

10. OCTOBER: BEAR WITNESS

1. John 5:30
2. John 14:10
3. Matthew 19:17
4. John 5:30
5. John 14:10
6. John 5:17
7. Matthew 9:33
8. Matthew 24:44
9. John 5:30
10. Psalms 29:4, 5, 7–9, 11
11. Joel S. Goldsmith. *The Infinite Way* (San Gabriel, Calif.: Willing Publishing Company, 1956).

11. NOVEMBER: GRATITUDE

1. John 8:11
2. John 19:11
3. Matthew 6:33
4. Galatians 6:7
5. Matthew 6:33
6. Acts 3:6
7. Isaiah 2:22
8. Matthew 23 :9

12. DECEMBER: TITHING WITH MELCHIZEDEK

1. Matthew 2:3, 4, 8, 13
2. Matthew 2:11
3. Luke 2:13
4. II Chronicles 20:15, 17
5. John 5:30
6. John 7:16
7. By the author. Reprinted by permission from The Seeker, Perth, Western Australia, Christmas 1956.
8. By the author. Reprinted by permission from The Seeker, Perth, Western Australia, Christmas 1956.
9. Matthew 11:4, 5
10. II Corinthians 5:15
11. By the author (London: L. N. Fowler & Co. Ltd., 1957).
12. Reprinted by permission from the Science of Thought Review, Chichester, England, October, 1957.
13. John 18: 11
14. Zechariah 4:6
15. Matthew 5:39
16. John 14:27

Joel Goldsmith Recorded Classes Corresponding to the Chapters of This Book

Many of Joel Goldsmith's books, including this one, are based on his recorded classwork, which has been preserved in tape, CD, and MP3 formats by the Infinite Way Office in Moreno Valley, CA.

The listing below shows the classes related to each chapter of this book. For example, "#159-1 1956 Chicago Closed Class 2:1" means:

> The recording number is 159, Side 1 (**#159-1**).
>
> The recording is from the **1956 Chicago Closed Class**.
>
> The recording is Tape 2, Side 1 for the 1956 Chicago Closed Class (**2:1**).

The Infinite Way Letters 1957

1. Out of Darkness – Light
No tape source known

2. Major Principles of The Infinite Way
No tape source known

3. Understanding the Body
#113-1: 1955 Kailua Study Group 4:1

4. Resurrection

#151-2: 1956 Second Steinway Hall Closed Class 2:2

#124-1: 1955 Kailua Study Group 15:1

#68-1: 1954 Honolulu Lecture Series 4:1

5. The Christ, the Presence in You

#151-1: 1956 Second Steinway Hall Closed Class 2:1

6. The Secret of the Healing Principle

#113-2: 1955 Kailua Study Group 4:2

7. Supply

No tape source known

8. Your Names Are Writ in Heaven

#150-2: 1956 Second Steinway Hall Closed Class 1:2

9. The Prayer of Mysticism

#120-1: 1955 Kailua Study Group 11:1

#131-2: 1955 Seattle Private Class 2:2

#132-1: 1955 Seattle Private Class 3:1

10. Bear Witness to God in Action

#128-1: 1955 Kailua Study Group 19:1

#128-2: 1955 Kailua Study Group 19:2

11. Gratitude

No tape source known

12. Tithing with Melchizedek

#122-2: 1955 Kailua Study Group 13:2